WHAT DOES IT MEAN WHEN YOUR DOG . . .

Starts losing his hair?
Develops a ball-like lump under his skin?
Displays lameness in a hind leg?
Has a bent-looking or limp tail?
Appears confused or disoriented?
Becomes lethargic?

FIND ALL THE ANSWERS IN

WHAT YOUR DOG IS
TRYING TO TELL YOU

St. Martin's Paperbacks Titles
by John M. Simon, D.V.M.

What Your Cat Is Trying to Tell You
What Your Dog Is Trying to Tell You
Anti-Aging for Dogs

What Your
Dog
Is Trying to
Tell You

A Head-to-Tail Guide
to Your Dog's Symptoms—
and Their Solutions

John Simon, D.V.M.
with
Stephanie Pedersen

Produced by The Philip Lief Group, Inc.

St. Martin's Paperbacks

This book is meant to educate and should not be used as an alternative to proper medical care. No treatments mentioned herein should be taken without qualified medical consultation and approval. The authors have exerted every effort to ensure that the information presented is accurate up to the time of publication. However, in light of ongoing research and the constant flow of information, it is possible that new findings may invalidate some of the data presented here.

WHAT YOUR DOG IS TRYING TO TELL YOU

Copyright © 1998 by The Philip Lief Group, Inc.
Cover photograph courtesy of Super Stock.

Library of Congress Catalog Card Number: 97-40592

ISBN: 0-312-97287-3

Printed in the United States of America

St. Martin's Griffin edition / March 1998
St. Martin's Paperbacks edition / January 2000

10 9 8 7 6 5 4 3 2

To my wife Joanie,
my office manager Judy,
and my entire hospital staff without whose daily
support and encouragement I could never have
found the time or energy to complete this book.

Special Note to Readers

This book was written with the goal in mind of helping pet owners identify with their dog's health problems. It furthermore provides the pet owner with a general idea of what to expect when they take their sick dog to their own veterinarian for diagnosis and treatment. Finally, homecare tips that can be used until professional veterinary care is obtained are discussed.

Although Dr. Simon practices both conventional and alternative medicine at his own clinic, this book limits his discussion to the conventional approach to diagnosis and treatment as it would normally occur at most veterinary clinics. Certain recommendations for homecare using antioxidants, mega vitamin-mineral therapy, and a few herbs are the exception to this rule.

Contents

CHAPTER 3
Head and Neck • 22

Contents

CHAPTER 4
Eyes, Ears, and Nose • 36

Contents xiii

CHAPTER 5
Mouth and Throat • 56

CHAPTER 6
Hair and Skin • 65

Contents

CHAPTER 7
Nose, Chest, Heart, and Lungs • 84

CHAPTER 8
Abdomen • 112

Contents

CHAPTER 9
Spine, Limbs, and Paws • 146

CHAPTER 10
Tail and Anus • 166

APPENDIX A
Checklist for Good Health • 178

APPENDIX B
How to Perform a
Weekly Home Exam • 186

APPENDIX C
Breed Disease Predilections • 189

BASIC ANATOMY OF A DOG

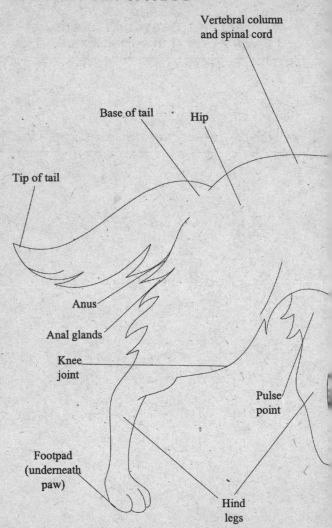

Vertebral column
and spinal cord

Base of tail

Hip

Tip of tail

Anus

Anal glands

Knee
joint

Pulse
point

Footpad
(underneath
paw)

Hind
legs

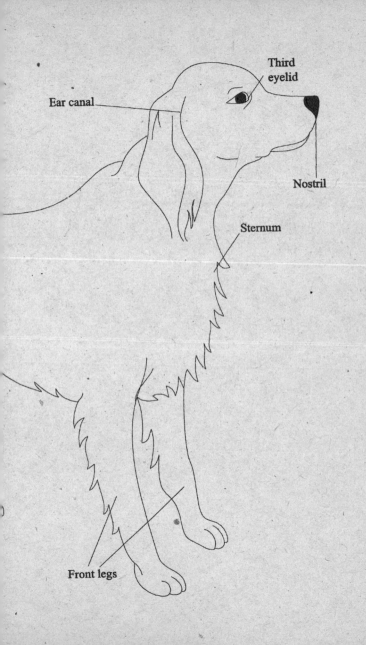

Third eyelid

Ear canal

Nostril

Sternum

Front legs

Introduction

Dogs are not like people when it comes to pain: They can't vocalize where they hurt, hazard a guess about what ails them, or explain the extent of their suffering. What they *can* do is give you certain physical signals that something could be wrong. Yet, how do you decode these clues to determine whether a condition is serious or not? At the first sign of something out-of-the-ordinary, should you rush to the vet in a panic and spend a good sum only to discover that nothing is wrong? Or is this the one time your hunch might be correct—and that immediate response is the only course of action that will save your loved one's life?

When something doesn't seem right with their pets, owners need quick, reliable answers that they understand. Enter: *What Your Dog Is Trying to Tell You: A Head-to-Tail Guide to Your Dog's Symptoms and Their Solutions,* an easy-to-follow medical reference written strictly for pet owners—not veterinarians. This is an important distinction; it means this book is designed expressly for those who have no knowledge of veterinary medicine but have a strong desire to help their beloved companions.

What Your Dog Is Trying to Tell You focuses on symptoms, those clearly observable tip-offs that something isn't right. To use this book, simply note your dog's symptoms, check the Contents to find your dog's most prominent symptom, and follow the page number to the corresponding section in the book. Find the entry that contains the combination of related symptoms that best matches those your pooch displays. Pointed questions about your pet's habits, age, sex, breed, and health history help guide you. Your answers act as clues to uncover what illness your pup may have, and also help you deduce how your pooch became ill. Accompanying the descriptive rundown of symptoms is advice on care and important information that can help you prevent the situation in the future. The extensive index also may help you locate more specific information.

Each of the chapters concerns a different region of the body. The book opens with a chapter on emergency symptoms—impossible-to-ignore signs that something is seriously wrong. Here is where you'll receive guidance on how nto handle crisis situations.

Chapter 2 covers behavior. Is your dog acting strangely—barking excessively, urinating on the rug, or lunging at the neighbors? This chapter can shed light on undesirable conduct and help you determine whether an illness or an environmental factor is to blame. You'll also find advice on addressing the predicament.

Chapters 3–10 address symptoms confined to specific body areas, including runny eyes in Chapter 4 (Eyes, Ears, and Nose) and loss of appetite in Chapter 8 (Abdomen).

Finally, convenient appendixes give you essential information at your fingertips. Here you'll learn how to perform a weekly home exam. You'll find a good-health guide that gives grooming tips, along with caring for a sick pooch, and other vital information. There's even an appendix listing canine breeds and the illnesses to which each may be prone.

In many cases, you'll definitely want to seek the advice of a professional veterinarian. And if you're ever in doubt about whether or not to call the vet, you'd be wise to call and check. But whether you're waiting to hear back from the vet or simply searching for ways to avoid future problems, *What Your Dog Is Trying to Tell You* offers easy-to-follow techniques to understanding your best friend's needs.

CHAPTER 1

Emergency Symptoms

Perhaps you've actually witnessed your pooch meet with misfortune, such as in a run-in with a vehicle, a fight with another dog, a fall, or taking a few quick sips of a poisonous chemical before you could stop him. Or maybe you've come across him after such a catastrophe. Either way, you're probably familiar with many emergency symptoms. After all, common sense is all you need to realize that if your pooch exhibits strong, dramatic signals—such as gushing blood, an exposed bone protruding from his thigh, an obvious wound, extremely heavy vomiting that seems unending, or perhaps even unconsciousness—you need to sprint to the vet.

Yet, what about those subtler signs of trouble? The ones that don't announce themselves, that maybe even show up gradually, but are every bit the emergency warning signs their more dramatic counterparts are? Sure, it takes an adroit owner—one who is thoroughly versed in her dog's normal behavior and vital signs—to spot anything unseemly, but most pet owners are just such people.

The point of all this is that just because the sign you happen to notice is subtle, it's still worth taking seriously. Indeed, some such signs, such as a change in posture, an unwillingness to move, a high fever, and unusually low body temperature, can all indicate life-threatening conditions, whereas other, more showy symptoms, such as coughing, sneezing, or loud wheezing, may indicate nothing more grave than a canine cold or a doggy allergy.

Abdomen: Acute Pain

You can tell your dog's abdomen hurts if he shrinks from being touched there, moves cautiously or not at all, or adopts an arched-back stance or prayer pose (back legs standing, front legs outstretched and lowered onto the ground, head resting on front legs). Other signs of abdominal pain include refusing food, trembling, vomiting, restlessness, whining, and labored breathing. The condition may come on suddenly. Because the source of the pain may be serious, **take your pet to the vet immediately**.

If you cannot get to the vet right away, there are a few things you can do to keep your dog comfortable. Try giving him buffered aspirin (¼ of a 325-mg tablet for every 10 pounds of body weight) or a baby aspirin (81 mg for every 10 pounds of body weight) 1 to 2 times a day. To reduce your dog's apprehension and discomfort, speak to him quietly and pet him in a reassuring manner. [Also see sections in Chapter 8, Bloated, Distended, or Painful Abdomen (pp. 112–113); Bloated Abdomen, Vomiting, Excess Salivation, and Rapid Breathing (pp. 113–114); and Obvious Bulge at Midabdomen, Groin, or Rectal Area (pp. 114–115).]

Bite Wounds

Should your dog get in a fight with another canine, give him a thorough once-over. Look for bite wounds. If left untreated, a bite can cause considerable blood loss. Plus, often embedded in such wounds are dirt, saliva, and hair from the rival dog—all of which can cause the wound to become an infected, abscessed mess. These contaminants can also cause blood poisoning. If the wound is bleeding, wrap it with a pressure bandage.

Don't try to wash out the wound yourself unless you are a long distance away from vet care. Instead, cover the bite with a clean cloth. If needed, apply pressure to slow the bleeding. Now you're ready to go straight to the vet. To prevent an infection, your vet will remove any embedded dirt and hair, clean the wound with a surgical soap, then flush it with water and a disinfectant such as 3% hydrogen peroxide. Finally, she will apply a wound antibiotic and bandage it. Antibiotics will be dispensed. The vet may recommend that you bring your pet back for a checkup in about a week, when a change of the dressing may be necessary.

Bleeding: Uncontrollable

Maybe your dog was cut by a piece of glass. Maybe he was hit by a vehicle. Maybe he snagged himself jumping over or squeezing through a fence. In any event, your pooch is bleeding and you want to make it stop.

Bleeding comes in degrees of seriousness. A relatively minor cut will typically stop bleeding by itself after 6 or 7 minutes. A larger cut might gush blood and may not stop bleeding without assistance from you. Find a *clean* rag, towel, or gauze bandage and hold it directly against the wound, applying pressure. If the blood flow stops, you can hold off seeing the vet for 4 or 5 hours, but **if the flow doesn't stop in 20 minutes, you must go straight to the vet**. After the vet has halted the blood flow, she will stitch the area closed.

You also must go straight to the vet anytime there is a deep cut in the dog's chest area. On the way to the doctor's office, apply a pressure bandage to the area. Should a rib protrude through the skin, avoid touching the bone with your hand or with the bandage. With a chest wound, you may notice air bubbles in the leaking blood. You may also hear a hissing noise: This sound is actually air escaping from the chest cavity.

If, for some reason, you can't get a wound to stop bleeding heavily after 30 minutes worth of pressure, and you cannot get to a vet immediately—perhaps you're camping or hiking in a secluded area—you may need to apply a tourniquet. Tourniquets are used *only* on appendages—in other words, the dog's limbs and tail.

To apply a tourniquet, find a soft, elastic fabric, such as a sock. Tightly tie the fabric around the appendage, directly above the wound. To avoid killing living skin and muscle tissue, you will have to loosen the tourniquet every 10 minutes, for 30 to 45 seconds at a time, to allow blood to flow into the appendage. Once the blood flow has severely slowed—or stopped altogether—replace the tourniquet with a pressure bandage.

Break, Fracture, or Sprain: Difficulty Moving

A collision with a car or bike, a fall—these can break or fracture a bone or injure ligaments. First, if you do see your pooch hit by a vehicle or involved in a serious fall, it's a good idea to take the animal to a vet straightaway for a checkup. Read the third paragraph in this section for information on how to transport an injured dog.

The more likely scenario, however, is that the dog was hurt during an unsupervised moment (for example, if you were watching the pooch, you probably wouldn't have allowed him near a moving car). Thus, you may suddenly notice your pooch limping (if a leg was injured) or adopting a hunched-up posture (if a rib was cracked or the spine damaged). You may also notice a cracking noise when your pet moves, as well as swelling at the injured site. You may even see a piece of bone protruding through the skin.

If you do see a piece of errant bone, you can be certain there's a break. Without visible bone peeking through, however, it can be hard for a nonvet to determine whether the dog has a fracture or has sprained or torn a ligament. Regardless of the actual problem, encourage your pooch to remain still while you muzzle him. This is important because a dog in pain will bite indiscriminately out of fear and discomfort. Moving him as little as possible, take your pet to the vet. How you move an injured dog depends on the size of the dog, the type of accident, and the degree of injury. If your dog is active but moves with a limp or carries a limb, then carefully lifting the dog into the car is fine. If the dog is unconscious, lying on his side, or just not willing to rise, using a rigid stretcher-like device is much safer than using a sheet or blanket as a "stretcher." Carefully sliding a board underneath the animal allows greater immobilization than a blanket. Splinting an injured limb is also advisable. Your vet will radiograph the injured limb, set a broken or fractured bone, wrap a sprain, or surgically repair torn ligaments.

Breathing: Extremely Difficult or Stopped; Unconsciousness

A breathing problem caused by a respiratory condition may not be an emergency. However, the following are cause for immediate action: If your pooch has had a run-in with a car or bicycle, consumed poisoning, or had a serious fall and is aggressively struggling for breath or has quit breathing altogether and lapsed into unconsciousness.

If the dog is still conscious, do not try to examine his mouth—you are likely to get bitten. **Get to the vet immediately**. If the dog is unconscious, ask someone to help you (if possible) so you can administer CPR en route to the vet. Place your hand in the mouth and throat to feel for any obstructions, including vomit, mucous, or blood. Remove anything you find.

Extend the dog's head and neck, take a deep breath (do not exhale), and close the dog's mouth. **Completely cover your pet's nose with your mouth, then exhale into his nostrils.** The air should reach his chest—watch for the chest to swell. Remove your mouth and allow the dog's chest to deflate normally. When it has, put your mouth over his nose and start again. This inflate-deflate cycle should be done 12 times per minute, until the dog begins breathing on his own.

Often, immediately after a dog has ceased breathing (or just prior to it), his heart may stop. If the nearest vet is some distance away, you also will have to perform external cardiac compression. Place the dog on his side, laying him on the firmest surface possible. Place your hands on the side of his chest, just over the heart (which is located just behind where the front legs meet the body), and press down firmly. Release. Then press down firmly again. Release.

Repeat until the heart begins beating. This press-release combination should be repeated a minimum of 60 times per minute. When you combine external heart massage with pulmonary resuscitation, you should produce 1 pulmonary expansion for every 5 cardiac compressions. This is difficult if only one person is doing CPR.

If yours is a giant breed, place the pooch on his back and press directly onto the sternum (breastbone) in the area of the heart. This can be scary because you may worry about breaking the ribs or causing some other type of damage. Don't—getting the heart beating is your first priority. Any resultant injuries can be addressed once the dog has been revived.

Burns

Dogs, being curious creatures, may find themselves face-to-face with spitting cooking grease, scalding-hot water, fire, scorching surfaces—even a caustic chemical substance, such as lye. If nearby, you'll hear your pooch's pained yelp, know that he's been burned, and you can immediately treat the injury. Because it's entirely possible that your pooch was burned while out of your sight, here's what to look for: Immediately after being burned, the area will be red and painful. If the burn is bad, the skin may even turn a shade of white or brown. The skin will be blistered and may appear shriveled. If fire or a hot surface caused the injury, fur may be singed or missing altogether.

Either way, as soon as you realize your pet has been hurt, cool the burn under cold, running water or use an ice pack or bag of frozen vegetables for 15 minutes. If you suspect a caustic material is to blame, go the cold-water route—it will help rid the fur and skin of any remaining chemicals. For acid burns, neutralize it with ¼ teaspoon of baking soda per pint (2 cups) of water. For alkali burns, neutralize with 2 tablespoons of vinegar per pint (2 cups) of water. Cover the wound with a clean, dry cloth or a gauze bandage and go straight to the vet.

Convulsions: Continuous

Your pet begins moving in a disjointed, jerky way. Suddenly, seizures take over his body—not just one seizure, but *one right after the other* with no letup. Your dog may (or may not) slip into unconsciousness, vomit, or lose bowel and bladder control. What should you do? Gently place a towel or thin blanket over the animal and **head straight for the nearest veterinary clinic**—even if it's not the one you go to regularly. Such nonstop seizures often lead to unconsciousness, then death.

En route to the vet, do not place your hand anywhere near your pooch's mouth—you can be severely bitten. And don't worry about whether your convulsing dog will swallow his tongue—it rarely happens. If you do suspect poisoning, be aware that you should never induce vomiting when convulsions are present.

Dogs who experience only one or two convulsions in 24 hours still should see a vet in order to get the condition diagnosed, but the condition is not an emergency unless the single seizure lasts for more than 10 minutes. While observing a dog having a seizure, make sure the poor animal does not injure himself against the furniture or any sharp object. Pillows work well to protect both pet and owner.

Electrocution

Puppies and untrained dogs love to gnaw on anything chewy—shoes, furniture, books, electrical cords. Although most of these objects won't harm your dog, chewing on electrical cords is a quick way for him to become electrocuted. (Less common causes include coming in contact with power lines, being struck by lightning, and touching exposed wires.) Typically, your dog doesn't chew on cords when you're around to catch him—which means you may enter a room to find your pooch lying on the floor unconscious, cord in his mouth. As long as the animal still has the cord in his mouth, he's probably still being shocked. **Do not touch the dog or you will be electrocuted, too!**

Instead, immediately switch off the electrical source via the circuit breaker. If, for some reason, it is impossible to shut off the electricity, use a nonmetal object, such as a stick, broom handle, or wooden chair, to move the dog away from the cord. If there is any water or urine on the floor, push your dog away from the liquid.

Another possible scenario may involve a cord lying next to your convulsing pet, who happens to be conscious. To distinguish this from an epileptic fit, look for pale burns around the mouth, surrounded by red, swollen tissue.

Check your dog for vital signs. If the dog is still conscious, do not try to examine his mouth—you are likely to get bitten. **Get to the vet immediately**. If the dog is unconscious and not breathing, ask someone to help you (if possible) so you can administer CPR en route to the vet. Start by opening the mouth and lying the tongue to one side, between the top and bottom molars. Place your hand in the mouth and throat to feel for any obstructions, including vomit, mucous, or blood. Remove anything you find.

Extend the dog's head and neck, take a deep breath (do not exhale), and close the dog's mouth. **Completely cover your pet's nose with your mouth, then exhale into his nostrils**. The air should reach his chest—watch for the chest to swell. Remove your mouth and allow the dog's chest to deflate normally. When it has, put your mouth over his nose and start again. This inflate-deflate cycle should be done 12 times per minute until the dog begins breathing on his own.

Often, immediately after a dog has ceased breathing (or just prior to it), his heart may stop. If the nearest vet is some distance away, you also will have to perform external cardiac compression. Place the dog on his side, laying him on the firmest surface possible. Place your hands on the side of his chest, just over the heart (which is located just behind where the front legs meet the body), and press down firmly. Release. Then press down firmly again. Release. Repeat until the heart begins beating. This press-release combination should be repeated a minimum of 60 times per minute. When you combine external heart massage with pulmonary resuscitation, you should produce 1 pulmonary expansion for every 5 cardiac compressions.

If yours is a giant breed, place the pooch on his back and press directly onto the sternum (breastbone) in the area of the heart. This can be scary because you may worry about breaking the ribs or causing some other type of damage. Don't—getting the heart beating is your first priority. Any resultant injuries can be addressed once dog has been revived.

If your dog isn't breathing and his heartbeat has ceased, alternate 1 artificial respiration with 3 heart compressions until reaching the vet—or until the dog's breathing and heartbeat kick in.

Fever

A dog's normal temperature ranges from 99.5°F–102.2°F. However, your pet's temperature can raise to 103.5°F if he has been exercising recently, is scared, nervous, or excited, or the air temperature is high. If your dog's temperature is higher than that—especially if he had a fever for more than a day—it is an indication that the body's immune system is responding to an internal threat or imbalance. Depending on what other symptoms your dog exhibits—these can be anything from coughing to lethargy, vomiting to confusion—he could have some type of infection, an endocrine disorder, cancer, a drug reaction, tissue inflammation, or an autoimmune disease. If your dog's temperature rises above 104.5°F, try giving him buffered aspirin (¼ of a 325-mg tablet for every 10 pounds of body weight) or baby aspirin (81 mg for every 10 pounds of body weight) 1 to 2 times a day. If his temperature continues to rise despite aspirin therapy, cold compresses or a cold-water enema (administered by your vet) may help bring the fever down.

Heat Stroke

Just like humans, animals who are left in hot environments too long are susceptible to heat stroke. Warning signs to look for include excessive panting, physical collapse, a body temperature as high as 108°F, and unconsciousness.

You can attempt to cool your pet down by immersing him in a tub of cold water, hosing him down, or giving him a cold sponge bath. Continue covering the dog with cold water until his temperature is below 104°F. **Get your pet to the vet as soon as possible**. The vet will combat circulatory collapse with internal drugs, and administer cold-water enemas to bring the dog's temperature down.

To prevent heat stroke, never leave your dog in a hot car. During the summer (or if you live in an environment that is warm all year), be sure your dog always has plenty of water to drink and refrain from leaving him outside in the scorching sun all day. If he must be outdoors, make sure that he can find a shady area to escape the sun and heat.

Insect Bites

Because of the amount of time they normally spend outdoors, dogs are prone to various types of insect bites or stings. You can tell your dog has been bitten by something if there is a swollen area on his skin or if he suddenly becomes weak (due to an allergic reaction to the bite). If your dog does grow weak, take him immediately to the vet. If the bite does not seem to have caused an abnormal reaction, you can soothe your pet's pain by applying a baking-soda paste (add just enough water to create a pasty consistency) directly to the bite or sting. If your dog has been bitten by a spider, the eye may be swollen shut or the whole side of his face may appear distorted—see your veterinarian. For more information about bites from ticks carrying Lyme disease, see section in Chapter 3, Swollen Lymph Nodes, Fever, Painful Joints (i.e., Lameness), and Neurological Abnormalities, (pp. 34–35).

Nails: Split or Broken

Although it might sound minor, a split toenail can cause your dog a great deal of pain. Signs that your pet is suffering from broken or split nails include limping and bleeding from the affected foot. Wash the injured toe with antibacterial cleanser, then wrap with cotton and adhesive tape. Take your dog to the vet, who may clip the nail past the split section, then cauterize the nail to prevent bleeding. If the area is not severely infected or swollen, you can attempt to cut your dog's nails at home. (See section in Chapter 9, Lameness in One or More Legs and Broken Nails on Affected Paws, pp. 155–156).

Shock

Shock is the failure of the cardiovascular system to provide the body tissue with oxygen. It almost always accompanies another serious condition, such as poisoning, physical injury, heavy blood loss, a severe allergic reaction—it can even appear after the dog has been weakened by a lengthy illness. Regardless of what causes shock, the result is the same: unconsciousness and eventual death.

Shock is a symptom umbrella, encompassing signals like quietness, inactivity, and ignorance of external environmental stimuli. Should any combination of these be present, take your dog's pulse. A dog in shock will have a rapid pulse that grows weaker as shock progresses. His heart and respiratory rates will also be rapid. Due to a lowered body temperature, legs and paws will grow cool to the touch. The gums may appear very red or pale, depending on the cause of shock.

If possible, press your finger against your pooch's gum. The area will blanch beneath your finger. In healthy dogs, the area will regain its normal color in 1 to 2 seconds. If a dog is in shock, the color will take longer to return.

However, you don't want to waste valuable time trying to diagnose your dog's condition. If you suspect he is in shock, bundle your pet in a warm blanket to preserve whatever body heat he has left and **immediately go to the nearest vet**.

Vomiting: Repeated; Diarrhea Due to Poisoning and Illness

If, after eating an unfamiliar food or garbage, your dog vomits 2 or 3 times during 1 hour or struggles with diarrhea, you do *not* have an emergency on your hands. If vomiting has only been going on for a short while, withhold all food for 24 hours. Rapid water consumption can stimulate vomiting, so limit your dog's drinking by providing ice cubes in place of water, or by placing ¼-inch of sugar water (mix 1 part maple syrup with 3 parts water) or carbonated soda (Coke with the carbonation shaken out, for example) in the bottom of his bowl (and wait 15 minutes before refilling an empty bowl). To soothe your dog's stomach, give him Kaopectate (1 teaspoon per 10 pounds of body weight every 4 to 6 hours) or Pepto-Bismol (1 teaspoon for every 20 pounds every 4 to 6 hours). If vomiting is due to consumption of a toxin, it may be best to allow the dog to vomit for some time in order to get the toxic substance out of the body.

If your dog is suffering from diarrhea due to poisoning or consumption of a toxin, fast your dog as directed in the preceding paragraph, but do not limit his water. A bland, cooked hamburger and rice diet can be served after the 24-hour fast. Activated charcoal (see Appendix E, List of Recommended Dosages, pp. 200–223) may be fed in an attempt to absorb toxins still present.

You *do* have a crisis when the animal vomits and/or has bouts of diarrhea continually for more than 24 hours, or if the dog vomits blood, passes blood in the stool, salivates excessively, or collapses, loses consciousness, has pale gums, has large pupils, or breathes rapidly. These commonly indicate poisoning or advanced stages of a stomach condition, such as gastritis, bloat, stomach ulcers, stomach tumors, intestinal foreign bodies, and intestinal obstruction (see Chapter 8, pp. 112–145). No matter what has prompted the symptoms, **you must get your dog to a vet immediately for diagnosis and treatment**. Dehydration can quickly result from repetitive vomiting and/or diarrhea, so wait no more than 24 hours before getting help.

CHAPTER 2

Abnormal Behaviors

There are two types of abnormal behavior in dogs: that which suddenly manifests itself in your pet, and that which may come naturally to a dog but is undesirable to us human types. Both are important to address. Because there's always an underlying reason for a sudden shift of canine conduct, the first scenario represents a change in the physical or mental wellness of your pet that, for health's sake, should be examined. A common example of just such an abnormal behavior is when a housebroken dog suddenly uses the living room rug as her personal restroom.

As for the second type of abnormal behavior, although it may seem like we humans are imposing our wills on our canine friends—and we are—it's important to keep in check many behaviors that may come naturally to our particular pets. Take aggression, for instance. Your pooch has to live in a world of humans, and if she lunges at, bites, or attacks a person—or a person's pet or property—her existence in the land of homo sapiens isn't going to be very agreeable.

Aggression

The term aggression refers to numerous behaviors—all of them undesirable: excessive barking, chasing, lunging at, and/or growling at humans and other animals; biting or snapping; and destroying property. An aggressive dog often exhibits a combination of these.

Many breeds—especially those known as watchdogs—are naturally aggressive. If not obedience-trained—either by you or a professional—German shepherds, rottweilers, Bouvier des Flandres, chow chows, Akitas, Great Danes, and many types of terriers continue to act on their natural aggressive tendencies. Attending puppy-obedience training classes is a good way to learn how to take control of a young dog.

Has your pet already graduated from obedience school? How old is she—and is she fixed? As an unneutered puppy reaches adulthood—and sexual maturation—she can become territorial and more dominant and protective. Although male dogs have earned a well-deserved reputation in this arena, unspayed females can be just as forceful—often barking aggressively, knocking down backyard fences, and destroying property when in estrus (in heat), and snarling and snapping when anything (real or imagined) threatens her offspring. Neutering your animal is the most effective way to curb such behavior.

If the aggression comes on suddenly, take a look at your homelife. Have you made any changes lately? Have you taken a job that keeps you away from home more? Have you moved? Have you had a baby or visitors with children? Do you have a new roommate—or even a weekend houseguest? Have you introduced a new pet into your home, such as another dog, a cat, or a rabbit? Dogs can be jealous and are creatures of habit—they don't like their routines upset. Aggressive behavior can be their way of telling you just how uncomfortable they are with any new arrangement. In the wake of any changes, spending extra time with your pooch is often a good start. Your vet can offer good advice on how to deal with such problems.

If nothing has changed at home, illness may be the culprit. Sudden aggression can be brought on by rabies or a condition affecting the brain, such as a brain tumor. Whatever the cause—breed disposition, sex, a change in environment, or a medical problem—your vet should be consulted. Aggressive dogs are dangerous. They can maul other dogs, trash collectors, meter readers, postal workers, neighborhood children—even their owners. If your pooch is ever involved in such a scenario, not only must you live with the knowledge that your pet has hurt someone, but municipal authorities may require euthanasia for your dog. An aggressive, dominant puppy is a potential time bomb. Unless you want a highly aggressive guard dog, consider having this pup evaluated by a behavioral consultant.

Apprehension/Timidness

Some dogs are timid due to their natural personalities. New situations make them shiver with fear; a visitor sends them running for the safety of another room; a Christmas tree or new piece of furniture prompts them to walk yards out of their way to avoid it. They may even display an exaggerated aversion to pickup trucks, brooms, or some other object. Perhaps the pooch was born that way, or perhaps the animal was abused or otherwise traumatized before you adopted her. Either way, interacting with such a dog in a soothing, kind, patient manner can help maintain her calm. If your pooch shies from a particular object, you might be able to counteract the situation. Introduce the object to your dog gradually—this may mean once every other day for a year—and reward your dog with affection or a treat when she doesn't run from it.

In an otherwise moderately outgoing or extroverted dog, apprehension typically signals illness. When something hurts—maybe due to a stomachache caused by gastritis, (an inflammation of the mucous membrane of the stomach), an ear infection, or even a dislocated limb—an animal will physically shrink from you, fearing you may try to touch the painful spot. A normally gregarious dog who hides or wants to be left alone is letting you know that she is not feeling right. Take your pet to the vet for a thorough checkup.

Confusion/Disorientation

In humans and dogs alike, confusion is a classic symptom of old age. If yours is a senior citizen, she may stand frozen in one spot—often with her head touching a wall—

wearing a dazed expression. To the human observer, it almost seems as if the animal has forgotten why she's standing there and can't seem to decide what to do next. Some owners report that their pooch will remain in this pose until she is gently coaxed to lie down. This stance isn't limited to time spent indoors: Your pet may suddenly freeze during a walk, too.

If mimicking a statue isn't disconcerting enough, a confused dog may be easily panicked by a sudden noise, person, or situation. When panicked, you can forget about your pet obeying orders—she's too busy scurrying around, literally trying to get away from whatever frightened her. To make matters worse, it's not uncommon for a disoriented dog to dart out, right in front of the car whose horn startled her, or smack into the large rival dog who spooked her. Considering the potential for injury, when outdoors, it's wise to leash a dog who shows signs of confusion.

Of course, old age isn't the only condition that causes confusion. Head injuries, concussions (see sections on Bleeding: Uncontrollable; Break, Fracture, or Sprain; and Breathing in Chapter 1, pp. 5–8), and brain disorders (see Chapter 3, pp. 22–33) also count confusion as a prominent symptom. Because they limit or distort a dog's contact with the world around her, illnesses that cause diminished sight or hearing—such as cataracts or a severe ear infection, respectively—can also be accompanied by confusion (see Chapter 4, pp. 36–55). Problems resulting in dizziness or loss of equilibrium (i.e., inner- or middle-ear infections) will also produce confusion.

Eating of Feces

Your pooch may voluntarily ingest her own or other animals' feces. She may also suffer from bad breath, vomiting, and diarrhea. Have you recently moved or made some other lifestyle changes that has upset your dog's routine? Has your pet been diagnosed with diabetes or a pancreatic or hormonal imbalance? A "yes" to either question may mean your pooch has **coprophagy**, a condition that prompts dogs to eat their own and other animals' feces. It should be noted that it is completely normal for a new mother to eat her puppies' feces, although in all other cases there is usually an underlying problem—either medical or behavioral—behind the condition.

Because ingesting the feces of other animals can put your pooch at risk for internal parasites, visit your vet, who will look for and address a possible underlying cause for your pooch's behavior. Remove the dog's feces daily from your yard. When on walks, keep your pooch leashed, which allows you to pull her away from any loose feces the two of you happen upon. Feeding her a digestive-enzyme supplement (see Appendix E, List of Recommended Dosages, pp. 200–223) may help solve the problem. There are also supplements that impart a repulsive odor/taste to the dog's own stool.

Inappropriate Elimination Habits

Anyone who has had a house dog knows this scene: You enter a room to see your pooch looking up at you, tail between her legs. She's feeling guilty about something, so you look around to find what that something is. Then you see it: A puddle on your newly waxed linoleum. Or perhaps you step in a damp spot while crossing the rug.

Puppies who haven't quite mastered bladder or bowel control and older dogs who are losing control of theirs are not exhibiting bad behavior. Pups—and young adult dogs who come from kennels or pounds where they were used to going inside—may take a bit longer to train. With any-where from 2 weeks to 45 days of continued training, the animal will master the art of "going outside." To limit damage to the home, an older dog with weakening bladder sphincter muscles may need an extra 1 to 3 trips outdoors each day. If the sphincter muscle becomes even weaker, the older dog may become incontinent and leak urine while resting or sleeping. (See section on incontinence in Chapter 8, Repeated Uncontrolled Passing of Urine in an Otherwise Housebroken Dog, pp. 123–124.)

Another case of nonbehavioral-based indoor voiding: an illness, such as a bladder infection (see Chapter 8, pp. 119–120) or diarrhea (see Chapter 10, pp. 173–177). In all cases of inappropriate elimination, it's smart to visit your vet for a routine checkup. He can diagnose and treat medical problems resulting in a lapse in bathroom habits.

Sometimes inappropriate elimination is a stress-relieving mechanism that relieves tension resulting from changes in the routine, such as a new job, which reduces the playtime the two of you used to enjoy. A new puppy or kitten can produce jealous tension in your other dog that can result in house-soiling. Moving to a new home can be upsetting enough to cause your dog to break house-training. Try giving your pet extra attention and a week or two to grow accustomed to whatever new arrangement has upset her in the first place. If, after 14 days, you are still finding puddles in your home, it's time to visit the vet—both for behavioral advice and a medical checkup.

Restlessness and Lethargy

Often there's a good reason your dog's activity level has gone up or down. Have you introduced a puppy into the household? Your grown pooch might be indulging in a second childhood now that she's got a playmate. Or, she could be physically hounding you (walking up to you repeatedly or standing up every time the new pup enters the room) because she needs reassurance that she won't be pushed aside. In the case of lethargy, a record heat wave could be the cause: You'd be taking things slow, too, if you were wearing a fur coat.

If you can't, however, find anything in the dog's environment—no change in temperature, no new family members, no change in schedules—to explain the change in activity, there very well may be an underlying medical cause.

A restless dog is a fidgety dog. She may pace. She may sit, then stand, then lie down every few minutes. She may make repeated trips to the window. This may sound especially familiar if your dog hasn't been fixed. An uncastrated male may detect a neighborhood female in heat and anxiously try to get out to find her. When in heat, a cooped-up female often paces, whines, and 'scratches at doors, trying to break free to meet a male. A dog who is restless, upset, or anxious could be hearing sounds of another animal outside in your yard, or perhaps a bird, squirrel, or raccoon in your attic. If your pet's restless behavior cannot be explained by any of these causes, your pet may be experiencing pain or discomfort from some internal medical problem—that is—nausea, intestinal cramps, muscle spasms, pancreatitis, or a ruptured disc.

Lethargy often looks like pure laziness, but it, too, can signal a medical condition. (Think of yourself: When you're not feeling well, moving around is one of the last things you want to do.) In fact, it's a common symptom that accompanies a large number of conditions, including neurological conditions (see Chapter 3, pp. 22–35), cardiopulmonary ailments (see Chapter 7, pp. 84–111), digestive and reproductive conditions (see Chapter 8, pp. 112–145), and bone and joint disorders (see Chapter 9, 146–165). It can even tip you off to your dog's diminishing sight (see entry in Chapter 4, 41–42). Before you rush to the vet, you should always check for additional symptoms. Is there anything else your pooch is doing that's not normal for her? Coughing? Passing a discharge from one of her orifices? Shaking her head? Make a note of these symptoms and then take your dog to the vet—the more information he has, the quicker and more accurate his diagnosis will be.

CHAPTER 3

Head and Neck

The immune system and the nervous system make up two essential parts of the body. The immune system, which stars the lymph nodes, works hard to protect the body from attack from foreign invaders—specifically, any illness-causing infectious organism. The problem with the immune system—from a dog owner's perspective—is that it works quietly. No high-drama symptoms here. If your pooch's lymph nodes are swollen, you won't know it unless you happen to run your hand over the area in a routine show of affection. This drives home the importance of taking a quick-yet-thorough daily inventory of your dog's health while playing with, petting, or grooming him.

The brain and spinal cord are known collectively as the nervous system. This network of neurons receives input from various body parts and from the outside world; it also transmits instructions throughout the body. These transmitted messages typically include communication between the nervous system and the outlying body parts regarding coordination, learning, memory, emotion, and thought. Though the signs of a problem with this system are a bit more obvious than they are with the immune system, they can still be overlooked. For instance, you may think that the odd head-cock motion that your pup has recently made a habit of is just a cute puppy pose; in reality it may be a symptom called head tilt that indicates a neurological problem—a problem with the nervous system's functioning. On the other hand, some neurological signs that appear quite dramatic—

seizures or fits, for instance—may actually be a passing symptom of unexplainable origin, which an owner may never see again.

Collapse and Narcolepsy

When the brain doesn't get enough oxygen, blood, or glucose (sugar: "brain fuel"), a dog can lose consciousness, a state that vets call **syncope**. The episodes are brief—usually no more than 1 minute—and are akin to human fainting spells. In the rare case that a spell lasts longer than 3 minutes, however, the dog can die.

Similar in appearance to syncope is **narcolepsy,** though the two conditions have totally different causes. Unlike the human version, when a person complains of excessive daytime sleepiness, a dog suffering from the condition often collapses to the floor from a standing position, where he will stay immobile and asleep for any length of time. As soon as the pooch is touched or spoken to, he "snaps out of it" and returns to a normal waking state. Typically, the symptom is inherited.

Brief Loss of Consciousness and No Response to Voices or Touch

RELATED SYMPTOM: The dog appears to faint and remains unconscious for only 1 to 2 minutes.

POSSIBLE CAUSE: Has your dog suffered from head trauma? Has he been diagnosed with low blood pressure, a heart condition, or a metabolic disorder? Is your dog a pug, boxer, Doberman pinscher, or miniature schnauzer? A "yes" to any of these queries may point to **syncope,** a condition where the dog loses consciousness due to temporary lack of oxygen or glucose to the brain.

CARE: Keep the unconscious dog warm and the environment quiet until the animal wakes up. If your dog wakes up fairly soon after his episode, make an appointment with the vet for an examination. However, if he is still unconscious after 3 minutes, carry him to the car and **take him to the vet immediately.** (To move a large or heavy dog, roll him onto a blanket, which can be used as a stretcher.)

To determine why your dog collapsed, your vet will perform a physical and neurologic checkup and possibly a radiograph, an electrocardiogram, a blood test, and/or a brain scan. Although pugs, boxers, Doberman pinschers, and minature schnauzers are prone to fainting spells, these spells may be related to conditions such as head trauma, low blood pressure, a heart condition, or a metabolic disorder, which can cause fainting. Treatment will depend on the underlying cause. Syncope is sometimes confused with mild seizures that produce unconsciousness without the more commonly associated violent jerking.

PREVENTION: Address all head injuries and blood, heart, and metabolic disorders promptly.

Sudden Collapsing to the Ground— Regardless of Where Standing—and Falling into a Deep Sleep

RELATED SYMPTOM: This can happen anytime: indoors, on a street corner, while playing with another dog, and so forth. A gentle touch or word rouses the animal, though if left alone, the pooch will sleep as little as 3 minutes or as much as a 2 hours.

POSSIBLE CAUSE: Is your dog a Doberman pinscher, Labrador retriever, or mixed breed containing one of these? He might suffer from **narcolepsy,** an inherited disorder of unknown origin that primarily affects these breeds. Narcolepsy is rare.

CARE: Narcolepsy itself is not inherently dangerous. The hazard lies in where your pooch happens to fall asleep, so be careful that your dog is not allowed to roam. A busy street or sidewalk—especially one far from home, which your dog arrived at while roaming—poses more of a threat than dozing off in the living room. If your dog is unconscious for a prolonged period of time, carry him to the car and take him to the vet. Should your dog be too large to lift easily, roll him onto a blanket, which you can use as a stretcher. If you can arouse your dog and coax him to stand, you can just walk him to the car.

There is no cure for the condition. Thus, your goal is to lessen the frequency and severity of the episodes. To do this, a vet may recommend low daily doses of a general stimulant. It should be noted that many dogs experience fewer narcoleptic episodes as they age.

PREVENTION: Although narcolepsy cannot be prevented, you can ward off injury by supervising your dog's outdoor play. If yours is strictly a yard dog, fit him with dog tags listing your name, address, and all pertinent phone numbers (yours and your vet's), so that if he happens to jump the fence and fall asleep away from home, there's a good chance you'll be notified.

Head Tilt and Lack of Coordination

Head tilt is a veterinary term describing a specific symptom that occurs when a dog tilts his head so that one ear is lower than the other. The eyes may move continually in a jerky, side-to-side manner. Head tilt is a specialized symptom and usually indicates a condition involving the **vestibular mechanism** (which is made up of nerves of the inner ear, brain, and spinal cord and controls balance and posture), and/or the **cerebellum,** the region of the brain responsible for coordination.

The dog can also be affected by related coordination symptoms: He may walk in circles (circling), lean on furniture or walls, stumble when walking, pick his feet up too high when walking (high-stepping), bob his head up and down when he eats, sway, and/or fall sideways when standing, and appear mildly to severely disoriented. In fact, the presence of jerky, excessive movements often signals a disorder affecting the vestibular system or cerebellum.

Frozen Facial Muscles, Stiff Gait, and Difficulty Moving Limbs, Neck, and Head

RELATED SYMPTOM: · Your dog's breathing may be labored although his appetite and eliminating habits will be normal.

POSSIBLE CAUSE: Are there raccoons in your area? Could your dog have recently come into contact with a raccoon? There's a chance he has **coonhound paralysis,** an uncommon condition that causes a dog's nerve roots and peripheral nerves (typically those of the head, limbs, spine, and nervous system) to become inflamed, making movement difficult.

CARE: Take your pooch to the vet, who will perform a blood test to detect the presence of coonhound paralysis.

PREVENTION: If you happen to live in an area with raccoons, supervise your dog's outdoor play. Hospitalization with nutritional support and possibly ventilation support (oxygen) may be necessary in advanced cases.

Head-Bobbing, High-Stepping, and Swaying When Standing

RELATED SYMPTOM: Your pet may also stagger and fall when getting up from a reclining position.

POSSIBLE CAUSE: Has your dog ever received a blow to the head? Has he been diagnosed with a brain infection or tumor? A "yes" to either of these may indicate **cerebellar disease,** a condition caused by any type of injury or inflammatory process involving the cerebellum (the part of the brain responsible for coordination of movement).

CARE: Take your pet to the vet, who will perform a complete physical and neurological exam, including blood testing and possibly a radiograph or brain scan to reach a diagnosis. If your pooch does have a cerebellar disorder, your vet will treat its underlying cause: for example, an infection warrants antibiotics, and a tumor can, in some instances, be removed. Anti-inflammatory drugs may be indicated to reduce inflammation and pressure on the brain.

Confining the dog to a safe area of the house will help avoid further injuries, such as falling down the stairs.

PREVENTION: There is no prevention.

Head Tilt and Jerky Side-to-Side Eye Movements

RELATED SYMPTOMS: In addition to head tilt, the dog may also lean on furniture or walls, stumble when walking, sway sideways when standing, high-step, and/or circle.

POSSIBLE CAUSE: Has your dog ever suffered an injury to the head that could have caused brain trauma? Has he been diagnosed with a brain tumor or ear infection? Is he an elderly dog? A "yes" to any of these questions may indicate a **dysfunction of the vestibular system,** a network of nerves in the ear, brain, and spinal cord that governs balance and orientation.

CARE: In mature animals, a vestibular condition will often disappear without treatment in 1 week. Still, it doesn't hurt to have your pet checked by a veterinary professional, who will use radiography and/or a brain scan to rule out a brain tumor or infection. The exact care your vet gives depends on what is causing the vestibular condition, although sedatives and indoor confinement may be prescribed to keep the dog calm and safe. Keep a close watch on your pet to make sure he does not hurt himself by bumping into furniture or falling down stairs.

PREVENTION: There is no prevention.

Staggering Gait, Moodiness, Aggressive Behavior, and Excessive Salivation or Frothing

RELATED SYMPTOMS: You may notice changes in your dog's personality. The dog may bark or bite without provocation, lose his appetite, stop drinking water, howl frequently, destroy property, act restless, and/or be overly timid. The dog will have an absent gaze and his pupils may be unevenly dilated. Physical signs you may or may not notice include a drooping lower jaw, excessive drooling, seizures, and wandering.

POSSIBLE CAUSE: Has your pet recently spent an unsupervised amount of time outdoors? Is there a wound on his body that could be the result of a bite? Has he been vaccinated for rabies? If not, he could have contracted **rabies**. The rabies virus lives in saliva, so in order to contract the disease, your pet must first be bitten by an infected skunk, bat, raccoon, neighborhood pooch, or wild dog. The virus works by attacking the nerve tissue, hence the disease's many neurological symptoms. The incubation period can be as long as 2 weeks or as short as 2 hours. Death usually occurs 3 to 5 days after the onset of symptoms.

CARE: Not only does rabies pose a threat to humans, but a loose rabid dog can infect several other neighborhood animals, sparking a mini-epidemic. If you suspect your dog has been infected with the virus, try to lure him to a secluded room and have as little contact with him as possible until you've called your vet and the animal-control officer. The local authorities will pick up your dog for quarantine and observation. If, after being watched, your dog appears to have rabies, he will die quickly or be put to sleep. Unfortunately, an autopsy of the animal's brain and salivary glands is the only way to know for sure if your pet had rabies.

PREVENTION: Make sure your pooch is vaccinated against rabies, and supervise outdoor play.

Wobbliness When Standing or Walking and Incoordination of Limbs

RELATED SYMPTOM: Your dog's head and neck movements may also appear uncoordinated.

POSSIBLE CAUSE: Has your dog recently been diagnosed with any of the following: anemia, a heart disorder, a respiratory illness, or a disc or cervical-cord disorder? Is your pet on antihistamines or anticonvulsants? A "yes" to any of these questions may point toward **ataxia,** a sign that reflects a problem in your dog's nervous system. Ataxia is actually a symptom, not a disease, which results from hampered communication between your dog's brain and body, making it difficult for the body to carry out any orders the brain makes for movement. The symptom is brought about by the trauma of a specific neurological illness or by a reaction to certain medications. Inner-and middle-ear disease can also produce ataxia.

CARE: Take your pet to the vet, who will diagnose the condition after performing a series of tests, including a neurologic exam, blood test, and radiograph. If a specific illness is behind your pooch's ataxia—for example, a degenerative spinal cord disease—that disorder will first be addressed. Generally, once that primary illness is treated, ataxia disappears. If a drug is the culprit, your vet will explore other medication options. Once you are home, take necessary measures to keep your dog from hurting himself by falling down stairs or bumping into furniture.

PREVENTION: There is no known prevention.

Seizures and Tremors

Seizures, fits, convulsions—call these episodes of uncontrolled movement what you like, they are still frightening—just ask anyone who has ever seen an animal or human in the throes of such a fit. In a generalized seizure, the victim stumbles to the ground, limbs stiffen and twitch, eyes roll back, the head shakes, the neck arches back, the jaws mash together, and drooling and loss of bladder and bowel control may occur. A local attack (a partial seizure) is limited to spasms of a single body part or region, such as the facial muscles, head and neck, the hindquarters, or just one leg. Fortunately, an individual incident is usually brief, lasting 30 seconds to 3 minutes or, in rare instances, from 10 minutes up to 1 hour. A dog may have only one episode during his lifetime, or he may have several distinctly separate spastic episodes over the course of 2 minutes, 2 hours, 1 time a week, or 1 time a month. Occasional mild, atypical seizures may show no muscle twitching and may appear as a momentary fainting spell.

·Should your pet have such a fit, quickly create a calming environment: Clear away all sharp objects, try to surround the animal with a cushion of soft bedding, remove any constrictive collars, turn off a loud stereo or TV, and keep your hand away from the victim's mouth (or you may get your fingers caught between teeth—and *no, your pet won't swallow his tongue*).

Animals rarely die during a seizure, although fits are considered life-threatening—and in need of veterinary attention—especially when a number of separate seizures are quickly repeated without the dog gaining consciousness between each one. Also, if a single fit lasts longer than 3 minutes, medical help should be sought. Wrap your pooch in a cocoon of heavy blankets and **go straight to the nearest vet clinic or hospital**.

As dramatic as this spastic display is, whatever prompted the seizure should concern you most. Of course, one major cause is **epilepsy.** Other illnesses connected with more generalized seizures include **liver** and **heart disease, metabolic-system abnormalities, brain tumors** and **trauma, infectious diseases,** and **poisoning**. When the seizure has passed—or during the episode if the convulsions are prolonged or repeating themselves—take your dog to the vet so that she can control the seizure and then attempt to discover what underlying condition has brought on the fit. (For information on **tetanus**, which can also produce convulsions, see section in Chapter 9, Stiff-Legged Gait, Incoordination, Weakness, Muscles That Appear Frozen, and Convulsions, p. 165.)

Convulsive Trembling with Stiffly Extended Legs and Upward-Arched Neck and Head, Accompanied by Falling Over

RELATED SYMPTOMS: If the dog is lying down, his legs may move in motions as if running. He may have compulsive chewing motions and may foam at the mouth. His pupils will be dilated, his tongue may be blue, and he may be unconscious.

POSSIBLE CAUSE: Is your dog a schnauzer, poodle, dachshund, beagle, Belgian Tervuren, cocker spaniel, German shepherd, golden or Labrador retriever, Saint Bernard, Irish setter, or keeshond? If the dog is female, is she in heat or pregnant? A "yes" to any one of these seemingly unrelated questions could indicate an **epileptic seizure**. Most fits last *no more* than 3 minutes.

An epileptic seizure by definition is a disease that has no underlying cause: It is simply a result of a misfiring of neurons in the brain, and it is diagnosed by excluding all other possible causes of seizure.

CARE: You don't have time to call a vet. Instead, immediately do whatever you can do to calm your dog, make him comfortable, and clear away any objects that could be injurious. Remove his collar if he is wearing one, turn off the TV or stereo to create a calmer environment, and banish children or any frantic humans (or pets) to another room. Avoid getting your hand near your dog's mouth—it could accidentally get caught between your pooch's teeth.

When the fit is over, bundle your dog in a blanket and take him straight to the vet, who will give him a thorough physical exam. If this is the first epileptic fit your dog has had, be aware that there can be future fits. Your vet may place the animal on anti-epileptic medication, which is usually continued for life. Your dog will probably remain tired for the rest of the day or longer.

Should you wish to treat your dog at home, you may want to try giving him an herbal treatment. Valerian, an herb with sedative properties, is useful for reducing anxiety and soothing the nervous system and treating muscle spasms (see Appendix E, List of Recommended Dosages, pp. 200–223).

PREVENTION: In dogs who have already experienced an epileptic fit, excitement seems to trigger repeat attacks, so avoid overly active play and overexcitement in general.

Spasms and Uncontrolled Movement of the Head, Eyes, and Mouth

RELATED SYMPTOM: Muscles of the area will twitch. The spasms may affect only part of the body (referred to as a partial seizure) or may spread to include the entire body.

POSSIBLE CAUSE: Has your dog been diagnosed with a brain lesion? **Partial seizures** are common in such animals.

CARE: During the fit, remove all sharp objects from the area and make your dog as comfortable as possible (see Seizures and Tremors, pp. 29–30). Once the seizure has passed—or during the fit if it is still going after 3 minutes—take your pet to the vet, who will perform a neurologic examination, radiograph, and/or brain scan to determine what is causing the seizure. If a brain lesion is what prompted the partial seizure, a veterinary neurologist will have to determine whether it is operable or not. If not, she will attempt to control the seizures with medication.

PREVENTION: There is no known prevention.

Tremors of the Entire Body

RELATED SYMPTOM: An important high-risk factor is a dog with a white coat.

POSSIBLE CAUSE: Is yours a young to middle-aged white dog, such as a chow chow, springer spaniel, weimaraner, dalmatian, or Samoyed? He may be suffering from **generalized tremor syndrome,** also called **white shaker dog syndrome.** A tremor is an involuntary movement of either the entire body or a part of the body. The action is constant, rhythmic (almost in a to-and-fro fashion), and happens while your dog is conscious. A seizure, on the other hand, can occur while the dog is unconscious.

Depending on the accompanying symptoms (such as apathy or change of posture), tremors usually indicate muscle weakness or a brain disorder. Note any of these additional signs and report them to your vet.

CARE: Take your dog to the vet, who will perform an MRI to determine if your dog does, indeed, have generalized tremor syndrome. If he does, your vet may prescribe corticosteroids, which keep tremors in check. You will also be counseled to avoid exciting the dog, which can worsen tremors.

To treat your dog at home, you can try giving him herbal treatments, such as valerian (which reduces anxiety and calms the nervous system) (see Appendix E, List of Recommended Dosages, pp. 200–223).

Swollen Lymph Nodes

When feeling achy and sick, how many times have you reached up to your throat to check the size of the glands tucked inside? What you're feeling for are your **lymph nodes.** These round organs range from the size of a pinhead to the size of an olive, and they are nestled under the skin at various sites throughout the body, including under the arms, behind the knees, and in the groin. These glands produce **lymphocytes,** illness-fighting white blood cells that produce antibodies and help protect the body from invasion by bacteria or other organisms. When busy churning out these warrior blood cells, lymph nodes often swell and become tender to the touch.

All this goes for your pooch, too. Enlarged glands—which you will probably notice while petting your dog—can mean your pup's body is hard at work-trying to fight off an illness. However, to find out what illness, it's important to check for the presence of any other symptoms and report them to your veterinarian.

Enlarged Lymph Nodes, Fever, and Lethargy

RELATED SYMPTOMS: The enlarged lymph nodes are most often found under the lower jaw, in front of the shoulder blades in the "armpit" area, behind the knees, and in the groin. Your dog may show no interest in food and lose weight. His abdomen may appear swollen and may be tender. He may vomit and/or have bouts of recurring diarrhea. He may also cough and have difficulty swallowing.

POSSIBLE CAUSES: Is your dog a boxer, basset hound, golden retriever, Saint Bernard, Scottish terrier, Airedale terrier, or bulldog? Is he older than five years? Your pet may have **lymphosarcoma,** also known as cancer of the lymph nodes. This is a type of cancer that metastasizes, which means it spreads to other areas of the body, possibly involving the chest, gastrointestinal tract, skin, eyes, and central nervous system.

CARE: Take your pet to the vet, who will do blood tests and/or tissue biopsies to determine whether lymphosarcoma is present. If it is, and if the cancer is limited to specific external lymph nodes, those nodes will be removed. If, however, the malignancies have spread, chemotherapy and/or radiation treatments will be needed to help slow down the cancer.

PREVENTION: Lymphosarcoma cannot be prevented. Chemotherapy is not usually curative but may extend your pet's life by about 1 year if discovered early enough.

Swollen Lymph Nodes, Fever, Painful Joints (i.e., Lameness), and Neurological Abnormalities

RELATED SYMPTOMS: Your dog may stagger when walking, have a stiff gait, appear dazed, and/or tilt his head. The dog's eyes may be inflamed. He may also chew or nip at his skin. You may actually see tiny dark purple-gray skin tags or mahogany-colored bugs, white dots, and/or black flecks clinging to individual hairs. There may be dry patches of skin or pimplelike sores.

POSSIBLE CAUSE: Does your pet spend time in wooded or rural areas? Have you recently found a tick on your pooch? There's a chance he may have contracted **Lyme disease.** This illness is caused by bacteria and is transmitted to dogs by feeding ticks.

CARE: If you suspect your dog has Lyme disease, take him to the vet, who will perform blood tests to discover the condition's presence. Antibiotics usually can eradicate disease.

PREVENTION: Have your pet vaccinated against Lyme disease and keep him away from wooded areas. Because infection does not occur until the tick has been attached and feeding off your dog's blood for some time, it's important to remove all ticks immediately (see Section in Chapter 6, Constant, Rhythmic Scratching, pp. 72–74, for tick-removing instructions) and dust the dog's fur with tick powder.

CHAPTER 4

Eyes, Ears, and Nose

As clichéd as it sounds, the sensory organs really are your pet's windows to the world around her. Given the importance of eyes, ears, and nose in your pooch's life, she'll probably let you know there's a problem as soon as she knows herself. For instance, if she gets a foxtail stuck in her ear, she'll give you clues to decipher—in this case scratching her ear and shaking her head in attempt to dislodge the irritant. Many symptoms may even be visually obvious to you, such as a discharge from the nose, waxy buildup in the ear, or a growth in one of the eyes.

Although conditions involving the sensory organs often come on suddenly, some develop gradually. Ailments involving the eye, such as cataracts and glaucoma, can be especially slow in evolving. Just like a human who is surprised during a routine eye exam to learn he has a worsening vision impairment, your pooch may have had enough time to adapt to the situation by the time you become aware of her severely hampered sight. Instead, you, the owner, should recognize clues when your once-athletic dog misses half the balls you now throw to her, or that she doesn't enjoy her late evening walks the way she once did.

Abnormally Shaped Eyes

A misshapen eyeball is a dramatic signal that all is not right with the eye. Perhaps the most obvious abnormality is the bulging eye. Though most notably linked with glaucoma, a bulging eye can also be a defect present at birth, or a side effect of severe dental disease. In rare cases, an eye may wither and become smaller, as in cases of **enopthalmos**. A bulging eye may also result from an abscess or tumor growing in the eye socket behind the eyeball.

In most cases, an abnormally shaped eye is an uncomfortable eye. Your dog may blink more than normal, have watery eyes, and in some instances experience vision loss. If an eye bulges or enlarges to an extreme, the eyelids may not be able to close and the eye will tend to dry out.

Enlarged Eyeball That Bulges from the Eye Socket, with a Dilated Pupil and Tearing

RELATED SYMPTOMS: The retina will have a faint green tinge. You may notice inflammation of the entire eye. Vision may seem diminished. The eye is often very painful.

POSSIBLE CAUSES: Has your dog ever been diagnosed with an eye condition, such as retinal atrophy or cataracts? Has she ever experienced an eye infection or injury? A "yes" to either of these questions may indicate **glaucoma.** The condition is caused by increased fluid buildup and pressure within the eyeball, which in turn damages the optic nerve and can result in blindness and the loss of the eye.

CARE: Take your pet to the vet, who may suspect the condition after a physical exam. He will then measure the pressure of the eyeball with a tonometer. Drugs may relieve the fluid buildup, and thus the pressure in the eye. Several surgical techniques, including cryosurgery (using liquid nitrogen to freeze the tissue), have been developed to relieve the intraocular pressure. Your vet may suggest removing the entire eye if it has been severely damaged by glaucoma.

PREVENTION: Address all eye conditions promptly. A red, inflamed eye (i.e., conjunctivitis) may be the earliest indication that glaucoma is present. The earlier the diagnosis, the better the chance to prevent the loss of vision and even the loss of the eye.

Eye Pops from the Socket

RELATED SYMPTOM: The eye doesn't actually fall out of the head, but is held in place by the lid.

POSSIBLE CAUSE: Is your dog a short-nosed breed or breed mix, such as a pug, boxer, bulldog, Boston terrier, Lhasa apso, or a Pekingese? Were you recently restraining the dog, grooming her, or applying any type of pressure to her head? Your dog may be suffering from a **proptosed eye,** a condition where the eye pops out of the socket.

CARE: Take your dog to the vet, who can diagnose the condition after examining the eye. If the eyeball has very recently popped out from the socket, your vet can push it back in place by hand. If some time has elapsed between the time the eye has left the socket and the time the condition has been discovered, there may be some inflammation or fluid buildup in the socket. Your vet will drain this, then put the eye back into place.

PREVENTION: There is no known prevention other than handling your dog carefully when restraining, grooming, or medicating her.

Cloudy Appearance to the Normally Transparent Front of the Eye

Eye conditions are quite common in dogs, especially older animals. In fact, there's a good chance that you've seen a pooch with an eye that appeared less than bright and clear: Perhaps a milky haze covered the entire cornea, or an opaque, off-white curtain covered the pupil and obscured the retina, or spots of white dotted the cornea. You may even notice a veil of black covering the cornea.

These **opacities,** as vets call them, primarily affect two parts of the eye: the **cornea** (the transparent tissue that covers the front of the eyeball) and the **lens** (a transparent biconvex sphere located behind the cornea and pupil that focuses light rays upon the retina). They can be white, gray-white, green-white, blue-white, yellow-white, black, or crystalline in appearance. They may be slightly see-through or completely opaque, and they can cover either the whole cornea or just bits of it.

Furthermore, these opacities may be: scars, in the case of eye injuries; inherited problems, such as **corneal dystrophy;** trauma or infection-related conditions that result in erosion or an inflammation of the cornea; or age-related problems, as in some form of **cataracts.** A vet needs to look at the eye to reach a diagnosis and devise a treatment plan, however, most of these conditions develop gradually and rarely qualify as extreme emergencies.

Cloudiness or Milkiness of the Normally Transparent Cornea (Corneal Opacity), or a Blackish Film Covering the Cornea

RELATED SYMPTOMS: One or both eyes may be affected and the opacity may also be accompanied by crystalline grayish, whitish, or silverish spots. You may notice tearing and redness of the eye. The dog might blink excessively and/or rub or scratch at the eye. The pooch may be very sensitive to bright lights. This condition is called a corneal opacity.

POSSIBLE CAUSES: Has your dog been suffering from an eye condition caused by a bacteria or virus? Has she ever experienced an eye injury? Does she ever fight with cats? Is she a German shepherd, French bulldog, Saint Bernard, Boston terrier, Chihuahua, dachshund, Siberian husky, beagle, or cavalier King Charles spaniel? Is she a short-nosed breed or breed mix, such as a Pekingese, boxer, or pug? Did one of her parents have corneal problems? A "yes" to any of these can point to any number of disorders of the cornea, including acute inflammation **(keratitis),** chronic inflammation **(pannus),** corneal erosions or ulcers, dystrophy, or degeneration. When the film is black in color, the condition is called **pigmentary keratitis.** It, too, may be caused by infection and inflammation of the cornea.

CARE: Although some corneal conditions are not sight-threatening, others can cause blindness if left untreated. Thus, it's a good idea to quickly see your vet, because the treatment depends on the particular condition that is causing the opacity. Corneal erosions and ulcers are first treated with antibiotics and then with anti-inflammatory eyedrops. If the ulcer resists healing, surgery to remove overlying dead tissue may be necessary. Thicker, more superficial opacities (such as pannus) can be surgically peeled off the front of the cornea. Corneal ulcers that heal may cause a permanent scarred area (an opacity) over the cornea.

PREVENTION: Address all eye conditions promptly. Keep your dog away from cats who might scratch her, high grass, sharp objects, high winds, and dusty conditions. When taking your dog for a ride in the car, don't let her put her head out of the window.

White to White-Blue Opacity of the Lens, Accompanied by a Dilated Pupil

RELATED SYMPTOMS: The lens opaqueness involves only the pupillary area. Therefore, it usually appears smaller and deeper than corneal opacities. The eye is usually not red or painful unless glaucoma accompanies the cataract. There is also little to no tearing.

POSSIBLE CAUSE: Is yours an older dog? Has she been diagnosed with a metabolic disease, such as diabetes? Has she ever been diagnosed with a prolapsed lens or retinal atrophy? Did one of her parents have cataracts? A "yes" to any of these may indicate the likelihood that the problem is a **cataract,** an ailment in which the lens of the eye becomes opaque, often causing blindness.

CARE: Have your vet give the dog a physical and ophthalmic exam in order to diagnose the problem. If the dog is elderly and the cataract affects only one eye, your vet may choose to leave the situation alone. But, because a cataract can grow to cover an increasingly large portion of the eye, your vet may want to remove it. Surgical removal of the cataract is now done with a hi-tech device that sucks out the cataract from the lens capsule. Dogs can see adequately without a lens, therefore there is no reason to have a prosthetic one put in (as is sometimes done in humans).

PREVENTION: Treat all metabolic diseases and eye conditions promptly.

Diminishing Sight

There are many types of blindness: partial, full, night blindness, **photophobia** (blindness in daylight caused by sun sensitivity), blindness in one eye. There are also many causes: hereditary, degeneration, infections, nutritional deficiencies, or trauma. Diminished sight can also be a secondary result of a primary eye disorder such as a cataract or **glaucoma**. Age is also a factor: As most adult humans know, sight becomes less sharp with time: the same is true for dogs. Both cataracts and **sclerosing of the lens** (a degenerative aging process that results in an opaque lens that is often confused with cataracts) are age-related problems that result in diminished sight.

If you notice your pooch bumping into things, not seeing movements in her peripheral area of vision, exhibiting difficulty with navigating in darkness or bright daylight, missing balls and other thrown objects during a game of catch, and hesitating to explore new or dark environments, her sight is probably failing. Blinking and squinting are also tip-offs to a vision problem. Visit your vet so he can determine what problem is behind your dog's impaired vision and whether the problem can be reversed—the latter depends greatly on the former. For instance, glaucoma-reduced vision typically improves once the glaucoma has been treated, but impairment caused by a retinal condition is often irreversible. If cataracts are removed, the dog's sight will improve, but it will still be far from perfect.

Blindness in Dim Light, Dilated Pupils, and a Marked Preference for Well-Lit Areas

RELATED SYMPTOMS: You may hear your dog bumping into things at night. You may also notice her reluctance to go out into the yard at night and a tendency to huddle near your legs in low light. In advanced cases, daytime vision might also be affected and you might notice your dog missing a ball or stick when playing catch. Symptoms usually appear between three and six years of age.

POSSIBLE CAUSES: Is your dog a Labrador, golden retriever, Shetland sheepdog, Australian shepherd, Tibetan or Sealyham or Bedlinton terrier, Border collie, Irish setter, toy or longhaired dachshund, toy poodle, Bernese mountain dog, or an American cocker or English springer spaniel? If so, your dog may have a disorder of the retina. These conditions are usually inherited and include hereditary ailments such as **progressive retinal atrophy** and **retinal dysplasia.**

CARE: Take your pet to the vet, who will examine the eyes and retina using a special instrument called an indirect ophthalmoscope. He may also perform an electroretinogram to diagnose a retinal condition. Unfortunately, most retinal conditions are untreatable.

PREVENTION: Although you can't prevent a retinal condition from affecting your dog, you can neuter your pet to ensure that other animals with a hereditary retinal condition aren't brought into the world.

Eye Area Growths

Bumps or lumps on the eyelid or lashline are usually one of the following: **sties, pimples, warts,** or **tumors.** They may or may not ooze a liquid, and most are slow in developing. Moreover, they rarely affect sight, but depending on how close they are to the cornea itself, they may irritate the eye and cause redness. These growths rarely constitute an emergency, but it is wise to have a vet examine and, if necessary, remove the mass.

One or More Red or Pink Lumps Along the Lashline or Eyelid

RELATED SYMPTOMS: One or both eyes may be affected and hair loss may occur around the lumps. The eye is normally not painful.

POSSIBLE CAUSES: These symptoms describe **sties, warts, chalazions** (swollen sebaceous glands of the eyelid), **cysts,** and **tumors of the eyelid.** They are not related or caused by any other diseases, and although they are found more often in the older animals, dogs of any age can develop such lumps.

CARE: Take your pet to the vet for a diagnosis. Care depends on what type of growth or growths your dog has. Sties can be treated with a regimen of hot compresses and antibiotic ointment. Warts and chalazions are usually surgically excised. In the case of tumors, a biopsy will be performed to determine whether the growth is cancerous— *most lid tumors are, in fact, benign.* If the tumor does happen to be malignant, your vet will probably limit treatment to surgical removal. Since cancerous growths in the eye area tend to spread slowly and invade only local tissue, chemotherapy is usually unnecessary.

PREVENTION: There is no way to prevent these growths. However, early detection when the lumps are very small makes for a more cosmetic surgical excision.

Eye Tearing

Eyes water when they are irritated. The cause of the irritation can be anything from a speck of dirt, to a sty, to an underlying medical condition. If the tearing is in both eyes and is the only noticeable symptom, the problem is probably not an emergency. Think back to what your dog was doing before the tearing began. Was she resting in a part of the house that was being cleaned? Was she outdoors during windy weather? Was she hanging her head out of the window of a moving car? If so, there's a good chance that the eye is trying to flush out a piece of grit. If, however, the tearing comes on slowly, is in one eye only, and/or is accompanied by any change in the appearance of the eye, or if there is a growth in the eye area, the problem may be more serious than a lodged speck of dust. Go to the vet as soon as possible—eyes are delicate organs, and eye problems can go from bad to worse very quickly.

When a medical condition is causing your pooch's eyes to water, you will often notice companion symptoms. Redness is often present. A red, inflamed eye can be the sign of a more serious problem. Pain as evidence by squinting or blinking should receive immediate attention. Carefully note any of these symptoms—they are what a vet uses to help distinguish one eye condition from another, and thus reach a diagnosis.

Last, if you have a light-haired dog, especially a poodle, you may notice that everyday tearing—for example, the kind prompted by a piece of dust in the eye—seems to stain the fur in the inner corner of the eye, directly under the eye socket. In most cases this is completely normal and does not indicate an eye ailment. However, it is possible your dog has a tear-duct obstruction, in which case your vet may need to flush the duct. In either event, you're bothered by how this staining looks, talk to your veterinarian. Low doses of antibiotics (usually given orally) seem to clear up the staining in some animals, though no one knows why.

Excessive Tearing with Sticky, Yellowish Discharge in the Inner Corners of the Eyes, Accompanied by a Number of Eyelashes That Appear to be Growing into the Eyes

RELATED SYMPTOM: Both eyes are usually involved.

POSSIBLE CAUSE: Do you notice lashes growing toward the eyeball? Your pooch may have **distichiasis,** a condition where, instead of growing away from the eye, eyelashes grow into the eye, causing irritation, inflammation, and infection.

CARE: Take your pet to the vet, who can diagnose the condition after a physical examination. The stray lashes will be removed using electrosurgery or cryosurgery (which kills the hair follicles) and antibiotics will be given to clear up any existing infections.

PREVENTION: There is no known prevention.

Excessive Tearing with Sticky, Yellowish Discharge in the Inner Corners of the Eyes, and Lower Eyelids Are Rolled Either in Toward the Eye or Out Away from the Eye

RELATED SYMPTOMS: Both eyes are involved. The conjunctivas will be mildly to severely inflamed. Tearing, too, may be mild to severe. The dog may also blink excessively and/or squint. If the lower eyelids roll inward, the eye slits will appear as if they are too small to hold the eyeballs. If they roll outward, the eye slits will appear as if they are too large for the eyeballs.

POSSIBLE CAUSES: Is your dog a chow chow, a type of hound, or a shar-pei? Or is your pooch a Saint Bernard, Great Dane, basset hound, type of spaniel, Bernese mountain dog, boxer, or mastiff? If you answered "yes" to the first question, your pup may have **entropion.** If you answered "yes" to the second question, your pet may suffer from **ectropion.** Both conditions are genetic and tend to occur in specific dog breeds.

In nonvet-speak, entropion means the eye slit is too narrow to hold the eyeball in place. To give the eye a bit more room, the lower eyelid rolls inward. Ectropion is just the opposite: The eye slit is a bit too large. Because it isn't taut, the lower lid tends to roll itself outward. Unfortunately, both conditions can cause irritation, corneal damage, eye infections, and conjunctivitis.

CARE: Take your dog to the vet for a diagnosis. Surgical correction of the eyelid deformity is the only permanent cure. In the meantime, if any infection arises, your vet will treat it by cleaning the area and giving you an antibiotic ointment to apply around the eye 2 or 3 times a day.

If you cannot get to the vet right away, clean the eye several times a day by flushing the eye of accumulated discharge and removing any dried discharge from the lids and corner of the eye. You can apply a few drops of artificial tears (such as methylcellulose, available at your local drugstore) to your dog's eye every 4 hours to offer her temporary relief until the vet sees her.

PREVENTION: There is no known prevention.

Excessive Tearing with Sticky, Yellowish Discharge in the Inner Corners of the Eye(s) and a Red, Inflamed Conjunctiva

RELATED SYMPTOMS: One or both eyes may be involved and the tearing, mucous, discharge, and redness may be mild to severe. The dog may also blink excessively and/ or squint. You may notice a protruding third eyelid, which can be seen at the inner corner of the eye.

POSSIBLE CAUSE: Was your dog recently exposed to a dry wind, either generated by the weather when playing outdoors or when sticking her head out the window of a moving car? Could she have been accidentally sprayed by pepper spray? Does your pooch have hair that hangs in her eyes? Has your pet been diagnosed with a bacterial eye infection or a generalized viral infection, such as distemper? Your dog may have **conjunctivitis,** a condition that literally means an **inflammation of the conjunctiva.** The conjunctiva is the normally pink mucous membrane that surrounds the eyeball. It can be irritated by a number of things, including dry air or wind, a particle lodged in the eye, or even a virus that has hit the rest of the body. Allergies are another common cause of conjunctivitis.

CARE: If the conjunctivitis is mild, you may be able to treat it at home. First, address the cause of the condition. For instance, if your pooch rides in the car with her head out of the window, keep the window rolled up; when the weather is dusty or windy, keep your pet indoors or in a sheltered area outside; keep soap away from your pet's eyes when bathing her; clip facial hair to keep it out of her eyes; and so on. Move your dog to a different location when you dust, vacuum, or cut the grass.

Clear away discharge 2 or 3 times a day using a soft cloth dipped in lukewarm water, weak chamomile tea, or a dilute boric-acid solution designed for opthalmic use (which you can purchase from your local drugstore). Then flush the eye with Visine, Murine, or artificial tears (such as methylcellulose) to help remove foreign debris and to lubricate the cornea in order to make your pet more comfortable. Covering your dog's eyes with a damp, warm compress can also be very soothing.

If the condition doesn't improve after 1 day of home-care, or if the conjunctivitis is severe, see your vet, who can usually diagnose the condition after a simple ophthalmic exam and a few simple tests. Should something be stuck in the eye, your vet will remove it. If the cause is an allergy, cortisone and/or antihistamines may be dispensed.

PREVENTION: Keep hair, soap, and foreign objects away from your dog's eyes. Don't expose your pet to dry wind or dust. Avoid running your pet through high grass. If possible, avoid those things to which your pet is allergic.

Opaque Film Covering the Inner Corner of the Eyeball, Accompanied by Tearing

RELATED SYMPTOMS: The eyeball may appear to bulge or shrink back into the socket. Blinking or squinting are often present. One or both eyes may be affected.

POSSIBLE CAUSE: Has your pet been diagnosed with a corneal ulcer or glaucoma? Could there be some foreign material in the dog's eye? Any of these conditions can cause the globe to be retracted and the third eyelid to be secondarily elevated.

An abscess or tumor of the eye socket just behind the eye may cause the third eyelid to elevate and become more apparent. Trauma to the eye can also produce a third eyelid protrusion. A loss of the sympathetic nerve stimulation to the third eyelid can cause it to protrude. This condition is referred to as **protrusion of the third eyelid.**

CARE: Take your dog to the vet. Treatment of an elevated third eyelid consists of making a diagnosis and eliminating the offending cause—that is—removing the foreign body or tumor or treating the ulcer or abscess. At home, you should flush out any accumulated debris and make sure that your dog does not hurt herself by scratching her eye: An Elizabethan collar can be used to prevent your dog from using her paws to rub her eye.

PREVENTION: Treat all injuries and infections immediately.

Swollen Red/Pink Lump Sitting Over the Inner Corner of the Eye, Accompanied by Tearing

RELATED SYMPTOMS: One or both eyes may be affected. The dog may also suffer from conjunctivitis.

POSSIBLE CAUSE: Is your pet a Pekingese, beagle, cocker spaniel, Lhasa apso, bloodhound, bulldog, or shih tzu? Is she two years of age or younger? There's a chance your pet may be suffering from a **prolapsed gland of the third eyelid.** The condition occurs when the gland that is located at the base of the third eyelid (which is thought to play a role in tear production) breaks loose from its attachment to this lid and protrudes outward so that it becomes visible.

The condition is also called **cherry eye** because the prolapsed gland actually looks like one of the small, unformed cherries that you sometimes see attached to another, fully formed cherry. It has also been referred to as a **haw.**

CARE: Take your dog to the vet, who will be able to diagnose the condition after a physical examination of the area. Treatment options include removing part of the gland or tacking down the migrating portion of the gland to the inner part of the third eyelid.

After surgery, make sure that your dog does not injure herself by scratching her eye: An Elizabethan collar is useful for preventing this. Keep the eye flushed of accumulated debris.

PREVENTION: There is no known prevention. The condition results from a congenital weakness.

Head-Shaking and Ear-Scratching

A dog experiencing ear pain can't talk to you about the discomfort. She can, however, let you know that something is wrong by shaking her head (in an attempt to propel the ache from the ear canal) or by scratching her ear(s).

If you see your pooch indulging in one of these behaviors, give the ear a look. Can you see anything caught in the canal? Is there any type of discharge or colored earwax? Is there a foul smell? Can you see very tiny, white, flecklike mites? Is there redness and swelling? Has the ear flap ballooned out and filled with fluid? If so, read on. Although some of these conditions can be addressed at home, others require the care of a veterinary professional.

Head-Shaking, Scratching of the Ear, and Tilting of the Head

RELATED SYMPTOMS: If the pain is mild, your dog may want her ears scratched more than usual; if the pain is severe, however, the dog may shrink from having her ears touched. The ear may smell foul and release a thick, waxy, yellowish or brownish discharge. The dog may appear lethargic, show a loss of coordination, stumble, circle to one side while walking, and exhibit a marked loss of hearing.

POSSIBLE CAUSES: Has your dog recently received an ear injury? Could a foreign body be lodged in your dog's ear, perhaps a foxtail that lodged there during an outdoor jaunt? Is your pooch a poodle, schnauzer, Old English sheepdog, or other breed with thick hair growing in the ears? Is she a dropped-ear dog, such as a beagle, bloodhound, or a type of spaniel? Is your dog bathed weekly or does she swim often? Could she have an ear tick (parasites that are especially common in the Southwestern United States)? Any of these point to an **infection of the outer, middle,** or **inner ear.**

CARE: If the pain and discharge are mild, and coordination and hearing seem normal, you can attempt homecare. First, look in the ear for a foreign object, which is most likely to be a foxtail or other plant matter. If you see an object in the opening of the ear canal, you can grasp it with your fingers or tweezers and remove it. To clean the ear, fill the canal with an earwax solvent and massage the ear vigorously. (You can either obtain an earwax solvent for humans from your drugstore, or ask your vet for one made specifically for animals.) Wait until she shakes her head, then use a Q-Tip or cotton ball to remove the debris that has been shaken to the surface. Once cleaned, isopropyl alcohol or 3% hydrogen peroxide may be added to serve as a disinfectant (which may sting if there are abrasions or raw areas in the ear). If the dog seems pained and resists homecare, take the pooch to the vet.

The vet will thoroughly examine the ear using an otoscope (the same device doctors use to look in humans' ears). If the dog is in pain or won't stay still during the exam, the animal may need to be anesthetized in order for the ear canal to be examined thoroughly. If fluid, excess wax, or debris is in the ear, it will be cleaned, flushed, and suctioned out at this time. Any underlying cause, such as mites, a tumor, or a lodged object, will be treated. Antibiotics will be prescribed to clear up any infection. Daily cleaning, applications of eardrops 2 times a day, and visits to the vet 1 time per week are necessary until the ear is totally healed. If, in spite of this care, the ear remains infected, an ear culture and antibiotic sensitivity test may need to be performed. On rare occasions, surgery may need to be performed to establish drainage or remove a tumor.

PREVENTION: Thoroughly check your dog's ears weekly and clean with an earwax solvent.

Vigorous Scratching of the Ears and Reddish-Brown to Black Earwax

RELATED SYMPTOMS: The ears may also be inflamed and the dog may frequently shake her head.

POSSIBLE CAUSE: Does your dog spend time with neighborhood canines? Do you own a cat? Your pooch may have **ear mites**—tiny spiderlike parasites. Though the pests themselves are hard to see, they prompt the copious formation of dark-colored earwax. To view the bugs, remove some of the wax from the ear canal with a cotton swab. If you hold the swab up to a bright light or smear the material on a piece of black paper, the mites will look like pinpoint-sized white specks (a magnifying glass is handy for this).

CARE: You have two options: Take your dog to the vet, or attempt to treat the mites with homecare. If you go to the vet, he will examine the ear with an otoscope and study the wax microscopically to determine the presence of mites. If the ear is badly congested with wax, your vet will thoroughly clean the area. A topical ear-mite formula and an earwax solvent will be prescribed, which you must administer to your pet daily, usually over the course of 1 month. Wash all bedding and vacuum rugs and furniture.

To treat your dog's ear mites at home, you must first clean the infected ear. Fill the ear canal with warm almond oil (available in health-food stores) to loosen wax and debris that have accumulated, then massage the side of the face just below the ear. After allowing several hours for the wax to soften, fill a large plastic eyedropper with equal parts lukewarm water and white vinegar and repeatedly flush the loosened wax from the canal. You can use cotton balls or Q-Tips to remove the debris that rises to the surface.

When the ear seems free of all debris, apply 6 to 10 drops of mineral oil to the ear canal: This will smother the mites. You should continue to clean the ear and apply the mineral-oil treatment twice daily for 1 month. If the problem persists for more than a month or recurs, see your vet.

PREVENTION: Supervise play with unknown dogs and cats. If you have a cat, have her ears examined for the presence of mites.

Violent Head-Shaking and Swelling of One or Both Ear Flaps

RELATED SYMPTOMS: The dog may also scratch her ear frequently.

POSSIBLE CAUSE: Has your dog recently suffered an ear

injury, ear infection, or other trauma to the ear? It is possible that she has an **aural hematoma,** known in layperson's terms as a **huge blood blister** on the ear flap. The condition occurs when a trauma breaks blood vessels under the skin of the ear, causing blood to accumulate between the skin and the ear cartilage.

CARE: If left untreated, a swollen ear flap can cause severe scarring and shriveling of the ear (cauliflower ear), so it's important to take your pet to the vet. In the event that you cannot get to the vet right away, talk softly and gently to your dog and use any other methods to keep her calm in order to prevent repetitive head-shaking or ear-scratching that can further damage the ear. Once you reach the vet's, a physical exam is usually enough to diagnose the problem. To treat it, your vet will lance the hematoma and drain the fluid from the ear, and then bandage or suture the area in such a way that the skin will be sandwiched to the cartilage.

PREVENTION: Address all ear injuries immediately. Clean the ears weekly to help prevent ear infections and violent head-shaking and ear-scratching, which can cause the blood vessels to break. Stop the dog from putting her head out the window of a moving car.

Nasal Sores and Nosebleeds

You probably already know a healthy dog's nose is usually fairly cool and slightly moist. But were you aware that a healthy nose has thick, even, intact skin? Should you notice a sore or scrape on the front of your pooch's proboscis, there's a good chance it was caused by something your dog did, such as rooting around a rough surface. Some autoimmune illness can cause a blisterlike rash on the nose or weeping sores around the nostrils.

As for nosebleeds, causes include a foreign object lodged in the nostril, a blood platelet disorder, and cancer. The blood may flow in a thin stream or it may be mixed with mucous. Unless you actually see something lodged in your dog's nose and can easily remove it (see the following), your best course of action is a trip to the vet for a diagnosis and treatment.

Abrasions and Scabs on the Front of the Nose

RELATED SYMPTOMS: The nose may be drier than normal.

POSSIBLE CAUSE: Has your pooch been rooting in rough soil with her nose? Has she been pushing her nose through the bars of her case or cyclone fencing? A "yes" to either of these questions points to a nose that has a **superficial wound.**

CARE: If the scabbing is hard and hornlike (which can indicate distemper; see section in Chapter 7, Constant Cough, Possibly Accompanied by Fever, Lethargy, and a Combination of Eye/Nasal Discharge, Diarrhea, Vomiting, and Muscle Spasms, pp. 94–96) or oozing sores appear around the nostrils (which can indicate an autoimmune disorder; see Chapter 6 pp. 65–83), a medical condition may be present: See your vet for a diagnosis and treatment. Otherwise, you can treat your dog's cuts and abrasions at home. To prevent scabs and/or abraded skin from drying out, rub a gentle oil—baby oil or massage oil will work—into the skin of the nose. If you fail to see an improvement in 3 days, see a vet, who may dispense an antibiotic ointment.

PREVENTION: Limit your dog's bone-burying activities to soft soil and attempt to teach her not to rub her nose on the bars of her cage or yard fencing.

Blood-Flecked Discharge or Pure Blood Discharging from One Nostril, Accompanied by Bouts of Sneezing

RELATED SYMPTOMS: The sneezes are often quite violent and recur in bouts of three or more.

POSSIBLE CAUSE: Does your dog play outdoors unsupervised? Are there foxtails and wild grasses, such as wheat, in the vicinity? It's possible that your dog has the **frond tip** of one of these plants **caught in her nose.**

CARE: If you can see the object protruding from her nose, gently and slowly try to pull it out. If the object is not clearly visible, try using a flashlight to look up into her nose. You can use a small pair of tweezers to gently grab any foreign object and carefully remove it from the nostril, taking care not to pinch any normal healthy tissue. If the object won't easily budge or if you are met with resistance once it is partially out, let your vet remove it.

If you can't see the object, it may be lodged deeper in the nasal cavity. Take your dog to the vet, who will thoroughly examine the area. In order to remove the culprit, your dog must be anesthetized, which will prevent her from sneezing or struggling. An endoscope may be inserted into one or both nostrils in order to see the offending foreign body.

PREVENTION: Remove all wheat grasses and foxtails from your property. Try to limit your pet's exposure to these grasses.

Bloody Nasal Discharge with Noisy Breathing

RELATED SYMPTOMS: Your dog may sneeze frequently and the nose itself may or may not appear misshapen. The blood may be from one or both nostrils.

POSSIBLE CAUSE: Is your dog older than six years? There's a chance she could have a **cancerous nasal tumor.** This condition usually affects older dogs and appears more often in long-nosed breeds, though all breeds and breed mixes can be affected.

CARE: Take your pet to the vet, who will give her a thorough physical. In order to confirm the existence of a nasal tumor, your pet will be anesthetized so that a tissue biopsy and X rays can be taken. Should cancer be present, your vet may remove the tumor and immediately place your dog on radiation therapy.

PREVENTION: Pay close attention to changes in your dog's nose and nasal secretions. Nasal cancer cannot be prevented, but the earlier it is caught and treated, the longer and more comfortably your dog will live.

Nosebleed, Accompanied by Blood in the Urine

RELATED SYMPTOMS: You may notice dark pigmented spots on the skin and mucous membranes. The dog's stool may be dark due to the presence of blood.

POSSIBLE CAUSE: Is your pet a type of poodle? Is the dog a female? Has your pet recently been diagnosed with lupus, a disease characterized by skin lesions? A "yes" to any of these may indicate a decrease in blood platelets. Known as **autoimmune thrombocytopenia,** this is a condition where the body destroys its own blood platelets, which are needed in order for blood to clot. As a result, capillaries hemorrhage more readily, and the leaking blood accumulates under the skin and mucous membranes.

CARE: Take your pet to the vet, who can diagnose the disorder after running blood tests. If the condition is mild, your pet may simply need corticosteroids, drugs that regulate platelet production. In more severe cases, your pet also may require a blood and/or plasma transfusion to increase the number of blood platelets.

PREVENTION: There is no prevention.

CHAPTER 5

Mouth and Throat

A slobbery welcome-home lick, a panting puppy at play, a dog riding in a car with his head stretched out the window and tongue wagging, a teeth-baring attack by an aggressive guard dog—a lot of the images we have of poochlike behavior involve the canine mouth.

A good rule of thumb when considering your dog's oral health is that many of the illnesses and symptoms that apply to you as a human also affect your pet. These include bad breath due to a kidney disorder or diabetes, problems with tooth enamel, periodontal disease, excess tartar, or an object lodged in the throat. Of course, you examine your mouth and teeth every time you brush your teeth. Although it doesn't hurt to regularly examine your dog's mouth and throat—even to give your pet's teeth a monthly once-over with a toothbrush—you must also be aware of signs that signal problems.

Bad Breath

Extremely bad breath (not the everyday doggy kind) may signal one of several things: **excessive tartar** buildup on the teeth, an **infection,** or a **tumor** somewhere in the mouth or throat. Bad breath can also be a result of certain types of food, **digestive problems, uremic poisoning** from kidney disease, **ketone breath** with untreated diabetes, and other metabolic problems. How can you tell the difference between healthy, pungent canine breath and the foul variety? There's only one way: Know the scent of your pet's regular breath.

Bad Breath and Excessive Salivation, Possibly Accompanied by Oral Bleeding

RELATED SYMPTOMS: Facial deformities may be present and the dog may have difficulty swallowing and chewing.

POSSIBLE CAUSES: Is yours an older dog? Is he a spaniel, pointer, or a short-nosed breed such as a boxer or pug? He may have an **oral tumor.** In elderly dogs, and in spaniels and pointers, these are quite often malignant. A benign growth, called an **epulis,** is common in dogs with short muzzles.

CARE: Take your dog to the vet, who will perform a biopsy to determine what type of tumor your pet has. Malignant oral tumors are fast-spreading tumors and quickly make their way to internal organs, such as the lungs. Benign growths require no treatment unless they hamper your pet's eating, drinking, or breathing.

PREVENTION: Check your dog's mouth regularly. You can't prevent a tumor from showing up, but you can prevent it from growing larger by taking your dog to the vet at the first sign of trouble. The earlier a malignant tumor is removed, the better the chances for preventing its spread.

Bad Breath, Swollen Gums, and Decreased Appetite

RELATED SYMPTOMS: Gums will be painful and might appear receded. They may also bleed. Your dog may stop eating altogether.

POSSIBLE CAUSE: Is your pet over three years old? Is he a small dog? Does he eat a soft-food diet and avoid playing with hard toys? If you answered "yes" to one or more of these questions, your pooch may have **periodontal disease.** The condition is actually extremely common—in fact, widely quoted statistics claim that 85 percent of dogs older than three years show some degree of the disease. In particular, small dogs are prone to the ailment.

The condition begins when plaque forms on the pooch's teeth. Humans brush this plaque away daily with their toothbrushes. Dogs, however, must rely on hard chew toys and crunchy dog food for this. These are very poor substitutes for brushing. If not removed, this plaque hardens into tartar, also called calculus, that attacks the gums (which may recede and bleed) and teeth (which may become loose and fall out). This makes for painful eating, and the animal may avoid food altogether.

CARE: Take your pet to the vet. If caught early, periodontal disease is easily treated with a dental cleaning not unlike those your dentist gives you. This is a job for a veterinary professional: Your pet will be lightly anesthetized during the procedure.

In more advanced cases, antibiotics will be given to wipe out any bacterial infection. Loose or severely decayed teeth will be immediately removed to prevent the roots from abscessing, to relieve pain that is likely to be present, and to reduce the overall bacterial population in the mouth.

PREVENTION: Brush your pet's teeth daily—you can use a soft, human toothbrush and doggy toothpaste from your vet—to help slow the progressive buildup of tartar and accompanying bacteria. To help strengthen gums and fight infection, give your dog vitamin C (see Appendix E, List of Recommended Dosages, pp. 200–223). You may also want to provide crunchy food and hard chew toys for your pooch to gnaw on.

Bad Breath, with Swelling Below the Eye

RELATED SYMPTOMS: The gum below the swelling may be very inflamed and the conjunctiva surrounding the eyeball may be very red.

POSSIBLE CAUSE: Does your dog regularly gnaw on hard bones, metal, wood, or rocks? He may have broken off a piece of tooth beneath the gum, which is now an **abscessed tooth**. When a tooth is abscessed, an infection enters the root canal through the break in the tooth, which can spread to the sinus cavity and to the entire jaw if left untreated.

CARE: Take your pooch to the vet, who will perform X rays to determine which root is infected. Depending on the condition's severity, the vet may remove the tooth or perform a root canal. Follow-up care entails 1 to 3 weeks of antibiotics.

PREVENTION: Limit your dog's chewing to hard chew toys and crunchy food. Brush your dog's teeth frequently and have his teeth cleaned at least once a year by a veterinary professional.

Difficulty Swallowing

Swallowing uses a combination of muscles, including the tongue, hard and soft palate, pharynx, and esophagus. Should a problem exist with any of these muscles, swallowing can be difficult. In vet-speak, this is called **dysphagia**. It can also be caused by a neurologic or muscular disease or a cyst, tumor, abscess, or even a piece of swallowed matter (maybe a twig or piece of bone).

Quite often swallowing trouble is accompanied by regurgitation, drooling, coughing, excessive head movements after chewing, a reluctance to eat, and weight loss.

Difficulty Swallowing and Chewing, with Either Fluid-Filled Swelling Below the Tongue or a Swollen Lump on the Neck

RELATED SYMPTOM: The area will be painful.

POSSIBLE CAUSE: Has your pet received a mouth injury from a bite, sharp bone, or blunt object? Your pooch may have a **salivary gland cyst**. When the salivary duct becomes injured and leaks, it can produce a blisterlike cyst. This swelling lump becomes large and inflamed and, on rare occasions, can turn into an abscess if left untreated.

CARE: Take your dog straight to the vet. After performing a physical checkup to determine the cause, the vet will drain or remove the cyst. She may install a drain to siphon saliva from the area. This will be removed when the stitches are taken out—usually 10 days to 2 weeks later. Following cyst removal, your vet may prescribe a week's worth of antibiotics.

PREVENTION: Prevent mouth injuries by eliminating

bones from the diet and avoiding encounters with strange dogs.

Difficulty Swallowing and Regurgitation of Food

RELATED SYMPTOMS: The regurgitation will be effortless and spontaneous, with no voluntary help from your pet. In other words, food will "just come up"—usually soon after it is eaten. Regurgitation should be distinguished from retching, which requires much more force and more violent movements.

POSSIBLE CAUSES: Such a situation usually results from a neurological disease that paralyzes the esophagus and causes it to enlarge. The condition, which can be inherited or appear as a secondary symptom of a **neuromuscular disease** such as **myasthenia gravis,** makes it hard for food to reach the stomach.

CARE: Watch the dog for 48 hours, feeding him water and semisolid food. If the condition does not improve, make an appointment with the vet, who will take a radiograph or use an endoscope to determine the cause. Some afflicted dogs improve with time, others need surgery to relieve the condition. Until your dog improves, your vet may have you raise your pet's front legs on a table or chair when feeding him so that gravity will help the food reach the stomach.

PREVENTION: There is no prevention.

Excessive Drooling and Salivating

Saliva—whether in dogs, cats, or humans—softens and lubricates food. Based on what we learned from Pavlov's dogs, it's not surprising that anything your pet connects with eating—a can being opened, the smell of dinner being prepared (yours or his), and so on—is going to prod his salivary glands to manufacture more of this sticky liquid.

Usually this saliva stays conveniently inside the mouth. There are instances, however, when it doesn't. In other words, the dog drools. Vets call this **ptyalism,** and it accompanies neurological conditions, such as motion sickness; gastrointestinal ailments, such as inflammation of the gastrointestinal tract; and metabolic disorders, like **uremia**. Because saliva helps cool the body, overheated pooches—due to either the temperature or overexcitement—often salivate heavily. So do animals who have ingested certain drugs or toxins. The condition can even be congenital, as in the case of giant dogs such as Great Danes, Saint Bernards, and mastiffs.

If the dog is otherwise healthy and the saliva is accompanied by no other symptom, try keeping your pet calm and cool for 1 to 2 hours and see if the saliva production slows down. If the saliva keeps coming, call your vet, who may opt to place the dog on a spittle-reducing medication. If left unchecked, oversalivating can cause dehydration. Be aware that in some cases drooling has nothing to do with excess saliva production but is a side effect of swallowing difficulties.

Drooling, Scratching at the Mouth, Choking Noises, and Restlessness

RELATED SYMPTOMS: Saliva may be tinged with blood and the jaw may appear propped open. The dog may experience difficulty swallowing, refuse food, paw at his mouth, and/or cough.

POSSIBLE CAUSE: Is your dog left unattended for periods of time? He may have swallowed **something**—anything from a rubber band to a fish hook to a small twig—that **has become lodged in his mouth, throat,** or **esophagus.** This could have happened moments earlier or weeks ago.

CARE: Take your dog to the vet. If an object isn't readily visible, a radiograph can help locate the culprit. This is important because the drooling and swallowing problems that accompany the ingestion of foreign objects are easily mistaken for rabies.

If something is lodged in the mouth, throat, or esophagus, your dog will be sedated and the object removed. Your vet will carefully examine the mouth for any resulting cuts, bruises, or abrasions. If infection has set in, your dog will be given antibiotics. After you return home from the vet's, feed your dog a soft-food diet for at least 48 hours to prevent irritating any painful areas in the mouth.

PREVENTION: Don't give your dog cartilage, vertebrae, or chicken, fish, or rib bones to gnaw on. Be sure all sticks you and your dog play fetch with are a type that won't splinter. (I have seen sticks and rib bones lodged between two teeth and across the roof of the mouth.)

Tooth Abnormalities

A dog's tooth is comprised of three layers: the soft, interior **pulp, nerves,** and **blood vessels;** the **dentine and cementum,** which make up most of the tooth; and the dense, brittle, white-colored **enamel,** which coats the tooth.

Like normal, adult human teeth, normal, adult canine teeth should show some degree of whiteness with no jagged or frayed-looking edges. They should be solidly anchored in firm, pink, nonbleeding gums. Obvious discoloration, abnormal positioning, a lack of uniformity, broken or loose teeth or bleeding or receding gums signal a dental problem.

Discolored, Yellowish Teeth

RELATED SYMPTOMS: The teeth will appear otherwise normal. Breath may or may not be bad.

POSSIBLE CAUSES: Is yours an adult dog who was given the antibiotic, tetracycline as an adolescent? Is he a pup whose mother received tetracycline? Does he have a buildup of tartar? Any of these can cause **yellow teeth.**

If tetracycline is to blame, the teeth are simply stained— they are perfectly healthy. If tartar is the culprit, be advised that if the buildup has been allowed to sit for an extended time, the teeth can remain somewhat discolored even after the substance has been removed. These cleaned-but-discolored teeth are also healthy.

CARE: With tetracycline-yellowing, there's not much your vet can do other than to assure you that your dog's teeth are healthy and perfectly functional. In the case of tartar buildup, your vet will clean your pet's teeth and show you how to properly care for them at home.

PREVENTION: Avoid giving young dogs tetracycline unless absolutely necessary. To prevent tartar buildup, brush your pooch's teeth daily (or at least weekly) and provide hard chew toys for him to gnaw on.

Jagged-Edged Tooth, Possibly Accompanied by Cuts in the Mouth

RELATED SYMPTOMS: The gums may be inflamed and sensitive.

POSSIBLE CAUSE: Has your dog been diagnosed with enamel hypoplasia (see Small, Underformed, Brownish Teeth in a Young Dog, p. 64)? Has he recently experienced some kind of trauma to the mouth—possibly a blow? Does he enjoy gnawing on extremely hard objects, like rocks? Your pooch may have a **broken tooth**.

CARE: Take your dog to the vet. If the tooth is free of decay, your vet may opt to simply file down the jagged edges. If decay is present, your vet may opt to fill the tooth or—if the damage is extensive—perform a canine root canal or extraction.

PREVENTION: Don't allow your dog to play with rocks. Should he receive a blow to the mouth or run into an object, check the teeth immediately for damage. Be sure to examine your pet's teeth regularly for abnormalities. A tooth may be broken horizontally (i.e., the tip breaks off) or vertically (i.e., a slice of enamel comes off the side of the tooth).

Single Discolored, Bluish-Gray Tooth

RELATED SYMPTOMS: The surrounding gum may be inflamed and/or painful.

POSSIBLE CAUSE: Do you not brush your pet's teeth regularly? Has it been more than a year since he has had a dental checkup? If so, your dog may have a **decayed** or **devitalized tooth**.

CARE: Take your dog to the vet, who will determine if there is a cavity or if the blood supply to the tooth has been damaged and the extent of the damage. The tooth may be dead. When appropriate, the veterinarian will treat the tooth with a filling, a root canal, a crown, or an extraction.

PREVENTION: Brush your pet's teeth daily. Do not rely on rawhide, Milk-Bone biscuits, or dry food to keep your dog's teeth clean. Annual to semiannual dental cleanings will help prevent cavities and periodontal disease.

Small, Underformed, Brownish Teeth in a Young Dog

RELATED SYMPTOMS: Teeth have a rough, coarse texture, and some may be broken.

POSSIBLE CAUSE: Has your dog had distemper before getting his deciduous or permanent teeth? Was he severely malnourished at some point in his puppyhood? If the answer to either of these is "yes," your pet may have **enamel hypoplasia**. The condition is marked by the incomplete development of the protective tooth enamel. It happens when the enamel-producing cells, called ameloblasts, are injured or destroyed prior to the appearance of the permanent teeth. As a result, the only part of the tooth that forms is the underlying dentine.

CARE: Dogs have much denser, sturdier dentine than humans do, so some never miss their tooth enamel. Others, however, miss it terribly and experience regular tooth breakage. If your dog is one of the latter—or one of the former and you'd like the teeth fixed for cosmetic reasons—a veterinary dental specialist can add a protective enamel-like layer to your dog's exposed dentine. Ask your vet for advice.

PREVENTION: If your dog shows signs of distemper (see section in Chapter 7, Constant Cough, Possibly Accompanied by Fever, Lethargy, and a Combination of Eye/Nasal Discharge, Diarrhea, Vomiting, and Muscle Spasms, pp. 94–96), immediately take him to your vet. Feed your pet a well-balanced diet of quality puppy food.

CHAPTER 6

Hair and Skin

Dense, shiny, well-conditioned fur and soft, pliant skin are hallmarks of good health for a variety of mammals, dogs included. But a beautiful coat counts for more than just decoration; it protects your pooch's precious internal organs from the environment and helps the body maintain a constant temperature.

Canine hair and skin are easy-to-monitor signs of your pet's overall wellness. Because a dog's fur and skin are among the last recipients of the nutrients she digests, failure to receive proper nutrition—or having an illness that leaches whatever nutrients she does ingest—can make the hair and skin go without their share so that the precious internal organs can receive nourishment. If this scenario continues, her fur and skin will suffer visibly. The hair may become thin or fall out altogether in spots, it may grow dull or become greasy. The skin may take on a different hue, turn dry, or become prone to infections—and these are just a few of the possibilities.

Hair Loss

Your dog's coat continuously replaces itself. At any given moment, there are hairs falling out, hairs growing in, and hairs that are resting beneath the surface, waiting for their turn to grow. Unfortunately, you can't determine whether your pet's hair loss is abnormal without first knowing what is normal. Although spring and fall are normal canine shedding seasons, it's common for indoor animals and longhaired breeds to shed year-round. In other words, if your dog fills a brush each day with shed hair and has always done so, that's normal. (Indeed, if your pooch is a heavy shedder, groom her daily to remove dead hairs and make way for the new ones. This will keep the coat clean and help prevent skin conditions.)

Keep in mind that normal shedding rarely produces bare spots or raw patches of exposed skin. Notice bald spots? Suspect a hair-loss culprit other than shedding. Hair loss, which vets call **alopecia**, can be motivated by numerous factors, including infection, pregnancy, parasites, malnutrition, trauma, stress, or a hormone imbalance.

Balding Torso, Flaky Skin, and a Potbellied Appearance

RELATED SYMPTOMS: Hair remains on legs and head, though the body may be completely naked. Skin is paper-thin, wrinkled, possibly darkly pigmented, and exhibits infected hair follicles. There may or may not be a marked increase in water and food consumption, elimination activity, lethargy, exercise intolerance, low body temperature, trembling, reduced muscle tone, eye problems, and/or bladder infections.

POSSIBLE CAUSE: Is your dog older than eight years old? Is she a poodle, boxer, or dachshund? A "yes" to either of these questions may indicate **Cushing's disease**, also known as **hyperadrenocorticism** or **hyperfunction of the adrenal cortex**. The condition can be blamed on the adrenal glands, which—usually provoked by a tumor affecting one or both glands—overproduce steroid/cortisone hormones. This surplus manufacture of steroid hormones by the adrenal gland can also be prompted by a tumor growing on the pituitary gland rather than the adrenal gland.

CARE: Take your dog to the vet. The foregoing signs can lead him to suspect Cushing's disease, but blood tests are necessary to confirm a diagnosis. One blood test involves injecting the dog with small amounts of synthetic hormones designed to alter the body's production of steroids and then measure the body's response.

Once a dog is diagnosed with Cushing's disease, a number of treatment options exist. The tumors accountable for Cushing's disease are usually slow-growing, prompting many pet owners to choose conservative treatment. Placing the dog on a high-protein diet helps offset protein loss caused by the disease. Secondary problems—such as bladder infections, skin infections, and eye conditions—are treated as they arise. Most dogs can live at least 2 years with this less-invasive method.

Another alternative is chemotherapy, which can be used to reduce the amount of steroids being produced by the adrenal glands. Applied correctly, this treatment can reduce or eliminate the clinical signs of Cushing's disease. Hair should begin growing back after 6 weeks; in 3 or 4 months, the dog will look normal. Although the dog's lifespan isn't necessarily shortened, therapy and follow-up blood testing are usually required for life. The most permanent, but difficult treatment option (and the most fraught with post-op complications) is surgical removal of the tumor.

Bald Patches, Accompanied by Scaly Skin, Heavy Scratching, and a Coat That Appears "Moth-Eaten"

RELATED SYMPTOMS: Hairless patches are most noticeable around the head, neck, eyes, ears, and/or feet. Sores, scabs, and/or pustules also may cover parts of the body.

POSSIBLE CAUSES: Does your dog spend time away from home in the company of other dogs (i.e., boarding, day care, or obedience-training)? Have you recently obtained a new pup? Your pooch may have **mange**. The condition is caused by one of several types of mites that burrow into the skin or live in the hair follicles. Depending on the type of mite responsible, some forms of mange can be transmitted to people and are intensely itchy. With **sarcoptic mange**, the owner may notice red, intensely itching bumps on his or her own arms or stomach. With **demodectic mange**, the itching is much less likely to occur.

CARE: Take your dog to the vet. To determine whether your pet is suffering from mange, and if so, which type, skin scrapings are taken from a few different body sites and investigated for mites under a microscope. An insecticidal rinse used every 1 to 2 weeks helps treat the condition. If the mite infestation is severe, an insecticide may be injected or given orally. Your dog will need to see the vet weekly or biweekly until the mange is cleared. Of course, if the dog's owner also has mange, he or she should undergo treatment simultaneously.

Mites are creatures that thrive when an animal's immune system is weak. Therefore, by enhancing your pet's basic diet with high-quality dog food and vitamin supplements, you can greatly encourage your pet's recovery. To help the body's immune system fight off infestation, give your dog antioxidant supplements such as vitamin A, vitamin C with bioflavonoids, vitamin E, selenium, sulfur, and zinc (see Appendix E, List of Recommended Dosages, pp. 200–223).

PREVENTION: It's difficult to prevent mites from using your dog as home base. You can, however, check your dog's skin daily. Anything unusual should be reported to your vet. Keeping your dog away from areas where lots of other animals congregate will reduce the odds of her contracting mange.

General, All-Over Thinning of Coat and Scaly Skin

RELATED SYMPTOMS: Fur is lackluster and its color may look faded. Any hair loss is generalized or symmetrical, but usually not patchy.

POSSIBLE CAUSE: Is it possible that your dog has internal parasites? Is your pet's diet of questionable quality? If you answered "yes" to one or both of these questions, the animal may be experiencing **nutrition-related hair loss.**

The old, dead hairs that your dog sheds are continually replaced with a supply of new ones. But if the body doesn't have enough protein and/or nutrients, it can't properly form these fresh hairs. Whether the body wasn't supplied with the proper protein and mineral building blocks in the first place or internal parasites are causing the malnutrition, the outcome is sparse, lackluster fur and dehydrated skin.

CARE: Take your dog to the vet. He'll review your pet's diet, check the animal for internal parasites, and arrive at the appropriate strategy.

You may want to give your dog mineral supplements containing zinc and sulfur, as well as vitamin B complex supplements (see Appendix E, List of Recommended Dosages, pp. 200–223), to further enhance the health of existing hair and to encourage regrowth in balding areas.

PREVENTION: To ensure your dog grows a thick, lustrous coat, ask your vet to recommend a high-quality, chemical-free diet that is high in protein and moderate in fat. Supplement your pet's diet with raw vegetables. Plant-derived digestive enzymes and omega-3 and omega-6 fatty acids (flaxseed oil) (see Appendix E, List of Recommended Dosages, pp. 200–223) added to the animal's diet will help encourage healthy skin and a full hair coat. An amino acid supplement would also be in order (available from your vet; a 20-pound dog gets ½ the recommended adult human dose. Also, have your pet checked at least twice a year for internal parasites—or immediately if you suspect something is wrong.

Small, Circular Bald Patches

RELATED SYMPTOMS: May or may not be accompanied by round, reddened skin lesions. The owner may also be infected with red, circular skin lesions.

POSSIBLE CAUSE: Has your dog come in contact with other dogs, cats, and/or pet owners? If not, has she touched soil that neighborhood dogs and cats play in? If you answered "yes" to either question, your pup may have contracted **ringworm**. The condition is not caused by a worm at all, but by any one of several highly contagious fungi. The name stems from the round, ringlike skin sores that often mark the ailment.

CARE: Ringworm is highly contagious. If you suspect

ringworm, try not to touch your pet until she has visited the vet, who will confirm the condition after performing a fungal culture. Treatment includes iodine or chlorhexidine shampoos, topical antifungal medication, and/or oral medications, such as griseofulvin.

Once you are home, you may want to shave your pet to make giving baths with the prescribed shampoos easier. (If you don't have the time to shave your dog or your pooch is uncooperative, you can enlist the help of a vet or professional groomer.) Vacuuming the house frequently to remove infected hairs will help to reduce the risk of reinfection.

If you are unable to get to the vet right away, and the ringworm is confined to just a few circumscribed spots, you may want to try painting the spots with tea tree oil (available at health-food stores).

PREVENTION: To stop a recurrence, wash and disinfect—or discard—your dog's bedding, collar, leash, sweaters, and grooming equipment. Since untreated ringworm spores can survive in dry environments for up to 4 years, disinfect all hard indoor and outdoor surfaces. Use 1 part Clorox bleach mixed with 10 parts of water to make an effective disinfectant that can be mopped and sprayed onto surfaces and used to soak certain washable materials. Fungal spores can also live in your heating and air-conditioning systems, so be sure to change all air filters. Enhancing the dog's nutrition and stimulating the immune system with nutritional supplements such as antioxidants vitamins C and E, selenium, sulfur, B vitamins, and flaxseed oil (see Appendix E, List of Recommended Dosages, pp. 200–223) is also important.

Thinning Coat, Extremely Flaky Skin, and Possible Darkening of the Skin at the Base of the Tail, Inner Thighs, and Armpits

RELATED SYMPTOMS: In addition, skin will feel cool, dry, and spongy and will be affected by an overproduction of sebum, a natural skin oil. Lethargy, fatigue, below-normal body temperature, increased appetite, and/or obesity may also be present. The condition usually does not cause scratching.

POSSIBLE CAUSE: If your dog's diet and/or routine has not changed but she has gained weight and has a thinning hair coat, your pet may have developed a **thyroid deficiency.** If left unchecked, a thyroid deficiency can eventually result in stunted growth, extreme obesity, a suppressed immune system, skin infections, and very possibly a premature death.

CARE: Visit your vet. To determine whether a thyroid deficiency exists, he will perform a blood test. To treat the deficiency, daily hormone tablets are prescribed. Your dog should respond to the medication within 3 weeks, becoming more active. Hair will thicken and return to normal in 2 to 3 months and excess weight will be lost. In most cases, thyroid hormones must be taken for life. Start by upgrading your dog's basic daily diet. Supplementing her diet with the antioxidant vitamins A, C, and E will help to slow progressive thyroid disease. You may also want to feed your dog a supplement of iodine containing kelp. (see Appendix E, List of Recommended Dosages, pp. 200–223).

PREVENTION: None. You can prevent the condition from becoming severe by immediately taking your pet to the vet when any of these symptoms emerge. A vitamin-mineral supplement containing iodine, zinc, copper, selenium, and B vitamins will help increase thyroid functions.

Scratching

Dogs scratch for a reason: They itch. But why they itch isn't so readily answered. Many once-in-a-while itches are produced by the very same things that make humans itch, from a moisture-sapping bath with harsh cleanser to skin-dehydrating central heating. Other reasons for a random itch include direct contact with hot or cold surfaces or a spot of pain.

You should become concerned when scratching is prolonged and/or furious. This scratching may be accompanied by biting or licking and often signals an underlying health condition or external parasites. Be aware that a dog's body takes only so much of this insult before repaying the assault with reddened skin, scaliness, localized hair loss, and infected sores in the affected areas.

Constant, Rhythmic Scratching

RELATED SYMPTOMS: The dog may also chew or nip at her skin. You may actually see dark purple-gray skin tags, mahogany-colored scurrying bugs, or black flecks clinging to individual hairs. There may be dry patches of skin or pimplelike sores. The skin is often red and traumatized by intense biting and scratching.

POSSIBLE CAUSES: Does your dog spend time outside? Is she in the presence of other animals? Do you board your animal, take her to the playground, or send her to obedience-training classes? She may be playing host to **fleas** or other external parasites, such as **ticks** or **lice**. External parasites are often visible on an infected animal—ticks can appear as plump, dark tags firmly rooted in the dog's skin and are sometimes mistaken for a skin tumor. These pests feed by biting the animal and sucking her blood.

In addition to being unpleasant, parasites cause skin ailments. The parasite bites the dog, the dog scratches—often so furiously that the skin is broken and made prone to infection.

Here's what else external parasites can do: These bloodsuckers can transmit germs and diseases—**Rocky Mountain spotted fever** and **Lyme disease** via ticks, for instance—into the bloodstream. A heavy infestation can cause anemia, which can be fatal if left unchecked. Also, some pooches are allergic to parasite—especially flea—bites: One nip alone can prompt a serious skin problem. Fleas are also notorious for transmitting tapeworms.

None of these problems are limited to just dogs. Ticks, fleas, and lice can affect humans in the same ways.

CARE: Suspect parasites? Thoroughly check the fur and

skin for ticks, fleas, and lice—and for their eggs and droppings. (Combing the dog with a flea comb can help identify parasites and possibly even remove them if they have not become attached.) Should you find your dog is infested, ask your vet to recommend a relatively nontoxic insecticide. Incorrect use of many commercial insecticides can lead to poisoning, so you should thoroughly read the label—most products call for weekly to monthly use. Many natural nontoxic insecticidal products are available, and it would be wise to try these first before using the more toxic chemicals. It is often the case that the relatively weak animals are parasitized, whereas dogs with healthy immune systems remain parasite-free. Providing your pet with optimum nutrition can go a long way in preventing parasitic diseases.

Treating the house and yard for parasites, especially fleas, is very important in the total elimination of these problems. Many types of foggers and housesprays are available, but I prefer the nontoxic powders that can be applied to the rugs after a thorough vacuuming. A once-a-month oral or topical flea preventive is probably the easiest, safest, and most practical approach. Other measures include bathing the dog every 3 days with d-limonene shampoo and buying a flea-and-tick collar. This will not totally eliminate the pests, but it will limit the number of them. (Be aware that care may differ if your pet is a puppy, or if there is a puppy or kitten sharing the house.)

If a tick is the culprit, remove it immediately. Generously soak the tick with alcohol or an insecticide, being careful not to get the liquid into your dog's mouth, nose, eyes, or ear canal and wait 5 minutes. (Avoid touching it: Direct contact with the bug may increase your chance of contracting a disease from it.) With tweezers, grasp the tick where it emerges from the skin and pull it out with slow, steady pressure. Jerking and twisting movements can break the parasite's body into pieces, increasing the risk you'll leave a bit of the bug buried in your dog, which, in turn, can lead to inflammation and infection. Check to see that the entire tick has been removed (you can see a bump in the skin if it is still there). If the tick is gone, wash the area with antibacterial soap and water and dab with rubbing alcohol to cleanse. If the tick has not been removed, call the vet, who will dig the tick out.

Don't limit treatment to the obviously infested dog. Any other pets in the home should be treated as if they, too, have external parasites. Clean all animal bedding every few days, vacuum your house thoroughly, and don't forget to treat your house and yard with an insecticide. Yes, these pests infest even the cleanest home. Fleas, for instance, spend only about 10 percent of their time on the animal. Therefore, if you treat the dog and not her surroundings, the pests will persist.

PREVENTION: Limit your pet's contact with strange animals and check your pooch and your surroundings weekly for parasites. Immediately treat infestations. Feeding your dog a high-quality diet and vitamin-mineral supplements (see Appendix E, List of Recommended Dosages, pp. 200–223) can help ward off parasites, who seek out animals with weak immune systems. Using a once-a-month oral or topical flea preventive (available from your vet) is the easiest and most successful method of flea prevention.

Intense Itching with Redness and Swelling of a Specific Area

RELATED SYMPTOMS: Signs usually are found on relatively hairless spots such as the chest, abdomen, and feet, but may be more generalized.

POSSIBLE CAUSE: Within the last 24 to 72 hours, has your pet come into physical contact for the first time with a "new" chemical substance, including (but not limited to) a cleanser, pet spray, insecticide, perfume, paint, or household solvent? Have you recently washed or treated your pet's bedding with a new product? Have you gotten new rugs? Yes? Your pet may have a **contact allergy**. A dog's fur acts as an armor to shield the body from contact allergens. Areas where hair is naturally thinner have less protection, thus they are more easily affected by irritants.

CARE: First, give your dog a good bath. Then make a thorough list of all new chemicals your dog has recently come in contact with. A list of chemicals that have never troubled him could also be helpful. Take these lists and your pet to your vet, who will work to identify the allergy-producing agent. (The list enables him to rule out any chemicals that your dog has possibly encountered with no adverse effects.) In addition to asking you to remove the offending agent, your vet will administer an anti-inflammatory injection to help relieve the itching and trauma. For your pet's relief, oral medication and skin lotion may also be dispensed.

If you cannot get to the vet right away, there are several things you can do to treat your pet at home. Bathe her with a shampoo containing colloidal oatmeal to alleviate scratching (available at any drugstore). You can apply a lotion containing aloe vera and chamomile to the inflamed sites and give the dog a chlorpheniramine (such as Chlor-Trimeton) or Benadryl antihistamine tablet to relieve further itching. Vitamin C, a natural antihistamine, can also be used with these medications (see Appendix E, List of Recommended Dosages, pp. 200–223).

PREVENTION: Keep all chemicals, including cosmetic items, out of your dog's reach. A new rug or carpeting has been known to produce contact allergies as well as fertilizer or weed killers. Even shampoos are suspect.

Obsessive Licking, and Perhaps Scratching, of a Specific Area

RELATED SYMPTOMS: If the licking has been going on for more than 3 or 4 days, you may find an irregularly shaped, vaguely oval, firm, plaquelike ulcer amidst a bald patch. The hair surrounding the affected area may also appear stained (caused by the saliva). The ulcers and bald areas are almost always found on a lower part of a leg, such as a shin or paw.

POSSIBLE CAUSE: Is yours a Labrador retriever, German shepherd, Doberman pinscher, Great Dane, Irish setter or other large, active, play-loving dog? Does she demand copious attention? Is she over three years old? Have you been spending less time at home? Your dog may have **acral lick dermatitis**, also known as **lick granuloma**. The disease can be triggered by simple boredom, but often the cause is difficult to determine.

CARE: Take your pet to the vet, who—in order to rule out other diseases—will perform a skin scraping or biopsy, study the animal's history, and note the ailment's clinical features. The most difficult part of treating this condition is stopping the dog from licking and scratching every time she becomes bored—so difficult, in fact, that many dogs are never cured of acral lick dermatitis.

Certain measures that help include spending more time with your dog, avoiding solitary confinement, and acquiring another (compatible) pet to keep your pooch company. In some cases, tranquilizers or antianxiety medications may be prescribed, and cryosurgery and acupuncture may be effective. Some owners think that the licking will stop if they put an Elizabethan collar on the dog; however, this is not advised because it is only a temporary solution to a long-term behavioral problem, and once the collar is off, the dog will begin licking again. Elizabethan collars may be advisable when combined with one of the other treatments listed above.

PREVENTION: Acral lick dermatitis isn't always preventable, yet commonsense measures like playing with and coddling your dog daily can help lower her chance of developing the condition. If you lead a life that requires you to spend time away from your pet, consider getting her a compatible canine, feline—or even a rabbit—pal.

Scratching and Biting of the Coat, Accompanied by Reddened Skin

RELATED SYMPTOMS: The reddened skin may feel abnormally warm to the touch. You may also notice small bumps, oozing areas, scabs, and/or dandrufflike scales. Areas where scratching is severe may become infected. Your dog may lick her feet and legs excessively, which can lead to a permanent reddish-brown stain on the hair. Head-shaking and ear-scratching are also very common. Watery nasal discharge, sneezing, and tearing may or may not occur.

POSSIBLE CAUSE: Does your dog have a known allergy—or possibly an unknown allergy—to a specific food, insect, chemical, or airborne matter? Her skin condition may be **allergic dermatitis**. There are dogs—just as there are people—who develop reactions when exposed to certain substances in their environment.

This exposure can be through inhalation (called **atopy**), ingestion, inoculation, insect bites, or direct contact with the irritating substance. If allowed to continue severely scratching, hair loss and a thickening of the skin can develop. (See section, Intense Itching with Redness and Swelling of a Specific Area, pp. 74–75).

CARE: Take your dog to the vet. To determine if an allergy is responsible for your pet's condition (and what that allergy is), your vet will run several tests. These include skin and blood testing. Skin testing involves injecting small amounts of common allergens under your dog's skin to note the reactions. Blood tests, such as the RAST (radioallergosorbent test) or ELISA (enzyme-linked immunosorbent assay) test, may be used in place of skin testing. Special elimination diets help pinpoint and treat food-related sensitivities. These diets, usually prescribed by a vet, contain only two ingredients—a source of protein and a source of carbohydrates (for example, venison and potatoes).

Your vet may recommend baths 1 to 2 times per week with a gentle hypoallergenic soap to remove allergens from the coat, help relieve skin inflammation, and prevent a secondary bacterial infection. If a secondary bacterial or yeast infection is present, antibiotics or antiyeast medication will be dispensed.

PREVENTION: Once you discover the guilty substance,

keep it out of your dog's environment. If it is not a substance that can be eliminated from the food or the environment, then it may be necessary to start your pet on a desensitizing series of injections.

Skin Abnormalities

True, your dog can't tell you what's ailing her, but that doesn't mean there aren't ways to tell. The condition of your pet's skin, for instance, says a great deal about her general state of health. A healthy animal has smooth, pliable skin. Her skin will have no excessive scaling, scabs, foul-smelling secretions, or parasites. Depending on the breed—or mix of breeds—the dog is, her skin will range from pale pink to medium brown to black. She may even have spotted skin.

Once a week take a thorough look at your dog's **epidermis** (skin). If you discover any unexplained changes— including some type of growth, sores flakiness, or abraded spots—call your vet. Many skin problems are easily explainable: Your dog was scratched by a neighborhood cat or tore a bit of skin trying to clear a fence. Other conditions can be caused by anything from a bacterial infection to a change in diet or environment to parasites. Some conditions can even be an external reflection of an internal disease.

Ball-Like Lump Under the Skin

RELATED SYMPTOMS: There may be one or more of these masses, most likely located on the head, neck, or back. A single growth can range from pea-sized to bigger than a golf ball, and can be moved with the skin (instead of being attached to the underlying muscle or bone).

POSSIBLE CAUSES: Your dog might have one of several types of **skin** or **sebaceous gland growths**. Skin growths are above the skin, whereas sebaceous growths are under the skin. These growths are quite common among adult dogs and are usually benign. Included in the noncancerous category are **sebaceous cysts**, harmless growths of the sebaceous glands, which are common in various types of spaniels, elkhounds, terriers, and shepherds. Unfortunately for boxer and boxer-mix owners, **skin tumors** within this breed are often malignant.

CARE: Because you have no way of knowing what type of growth your dog has or whether it's benign or malignant, your pet must visit the vet. He will remove the mass and send it out to a laboratory, where a histopathology will be performed to determine what type of growth it is. Homecare includes cleaning the incision 2 times a day and returning in 10 days to have stitches removed.

PREVENTION: You can't prevent tumors or cysts, but you can keep them from growing worse. See a vet upon discovering one and *do not squeeze* or try to "pop" the lump (it isn't a pimple). Local pressure can irritate and inflame the skin.

Broken, Reddened Skin, Accompanied by Pimples, Pustules, and/or Dry, Crusty Patches

RELATED SYMPTOMS: Skin might be weeping and you may notice flakiness. There may be mild to severe scratching and spots of hair loss. Small pimples may be noticed: These pimples may actually be small pustules that break open when scratched.

POSSIBLE CAUSES: Has your dog recently been treated for external parasites? Does she come in regular contact with other canines? Or does she have an allergic, hormonal, or immune-system malfunction? Is her diet unbalanced? If your dog fits into any one of these seemingly unrelated categories, she could have one of several **bacterial skin diseases**.

Dogs aren't usually struck by bacterial skin diseases unless there is some underlying health disorder that lowers their skin defenses. When this fortification goes down, the disease-causing bacteria found naturally in the environment seize the chance to play house and multiply on your dog's skin. Many of these diseases—**folliculitis, canine acne** in juvenile pups, and **impetigo** (milk rash) in puppies—have human counterparts.

CARE: Bacterial skin conditions are usually limited to the skin's outermost layers. If left untreated, however, they can spread to the deeper layers, hampering treatment. Take your animal to the vet, who will prescribe oral antibiotics and nutritional supplements.

To promote healing, keep skin lesions clean and dry. Your vet may prescribe daily applications of antibiotic ointment and semiweekly to weekly baths with medicated shampoo.

If you would like to try to treat a bacterial skin disease at home before going to the vet or you are unable to get to the vet right away, you can apply soothing, anti-inflammatory, antibacterial sprays (containing tea tree oil, aloe vera, and chamomile) to the most inflamed areas several times a day. Washing your dog 2 times a week with sulfur-based shampoo, immediately followed by an oatmeal rinse containing moisturizers, is the best way to treat a generalized bacterial infection that affects many areas of the body. (These products can be obtained at your vet clinic.)

Add vitamins C and E as well as zinc and sulfur to your dog's diet. Proteolytic plant-enzyme dietary supplements give the immune system strength and are very effective. If an allergy is the underlying cause of the bacterial infection, you should also switch your pet's diet to a high-quality, chemical-free one with lamb and rice or venison and potato in place of beef.

PREVENTION: Carefully monitoring your pet's health and maintaining it with the proper nutrition will result in a strong immune system that will resist bacterial invasion.

Extremely Dry, Crusty Skin with Grayish-White Flakes and a Dry, Dull Coat or Waxy, Crusty Skin with Yellowish Flakes and Rancid Odor

RELATED SYMPTOMS: There may be extremely mild to moderate itching. Broken skin and varying degrees of hair loss due to scratching may be present. The outer ear may be waxy and inflamed.

POSSIBLE CAUSE: Does your dog's thyroid function poorly? Or does she have allergies? Or has she been diagnosed with cancer? Or is she one of the following breeds (or a mix containing one of these): spaniel, West Highland white terrier, basset hound, dachshund, golden retriever, shar-pei, Doberman pinscher, Irish setter, or German shepherd? If so, then your pet may have **seborrhea**. The condition also affects humans (but is not contagious between dogs and humans) and is an illness that can manifest itself in either of two ways: Marked by an abnormal skin-cell turnover rate, this off-kilter skin cell production can, in turn, lead to either excessive dryness or excessive oil-gland production.

Seborrhea can be caused by a number of diseases, yet it also shows up on its own—especially in the breeds mentioned.

CARE: Take your pooch to the vet. Diagnosing seborrhea isn't especially difficult, yet determining why the dog has the condition can be. Your vet will run a series of tests (e.g., a thyroid function, allergy testing, bacterial culture, a skin biopsy, etc.) to determine whether the seborrhea is your pet's only condition or whether it is a result of another illness. If it is secondary, the underlying disease will be treated first, then your vet will treat the seborrhea.

The latter usually entails washing 1 to 2 times a week with medicated shampoos containing chlorhexidine, salicylic acid, tar, sulfur, and/or selenium disulfide. If the pooch's seborrhea is of the dry variety, your vet will prescribe following the bath with a moisturizing skin rinse and may prescribe fatty-acid supplements. You may want to add vitamins C and E, zinc, and sulfur to your dog's diet, as well as a plant-enzyme dietary supplement containing high levels of lipase. (see Appendix E, List of Recommended Dosages, pp. 200–223).

PREVENTION: When seborrhea is caused by another ill-

ness, prompt attention to that condition can prevent seborrhea from becoming even more entrenched.

Large, Fluctuant Bump That Feels Warm and Pains the Dog When Touched

RELATED SYMPTOMS: The area is red, swollen, and inflamed. The dog may have a fever, seem depressed, and/or
uninterested in food.

POSSIBLE CAUSE: Has your dog been bitten or otherwise wounded recently? If the site has become infected a
skin abscess may have developed. Abscesses are formed
when bacteria infects a wound, destroying underlying tissue
and creating a cavity where pus collects. If the dog has an
inefficient immune system or the invading bacteria is especially hardy, the infection may reach the bloodstream,
where it can poison the blood and eventually lead to death.

CARE: If you are not able to get to the vet for a while,
you can try to treat your dog at home. Soak the abscess
with hot compresses until it "points" and eventually opens
and drains. Flush the abscess with 3% hydrogen peroxide,
and fill the abscess pocket with colloidal silver 3 times a
day. Keep the wound open and continue flushing and medicating for at least 4 days. You can supplement your dog's
diet with oral proteolytic plant enzymes, zinc, sulfur, vitamin E, and vitamin C (all of which help support the immune system). The herb Echinacea can be given orally as
an antibacterial remedy (see Appendix E, List of Recommended Dosages, pp. 200–223).

If, after attempting homecare, the abscess is not healing
or appears infected, take your dog to the vet. If the bump
is an abscess, but is not ready to lance, your vet may ask
you to place a warm poultice or washcloth on the spot
several times a day. This helps localize the infection for
more effective drainage.

After draining the abscess—or if it has burst before ar-
riving at the vet's—your vet will probe, clean, flush, and

medicate the abscess's crater so it can heal. The opening created for drainage usually will not be sutured closed, but left open. Oral antibiotics are usually prescribed, as well as an antibacterial solution that the owner will use to further flush the abscess at home.

PREVENTION: Immediately flush and clean all wounds with mild soap and large amounts of warm, clean water. Using 3% hydrogen peroxide is good for flushing and disinfecting. Cat bites are particularly likely to produce abscesses because the bite wounds are so tiny that they are difficult to flush, so keep your dog away from aggressive neighborhood cats.

CHAPTER 7

Nose, Chest, Heart, and Lungs

Your dog's cardiopulmonary system—known as the circulatory and respiratory systems, respectively—is a vast network of blood vessels and major organs, including the heart and lungs. Because this part of your pet's anatomy so closely resembles your own, you will probably recognize any corresponding symptoms that broadcast your dog is ill.

As they would with a human, problems involving the respiratory system often have very noticeable signs—namely, labored breathing and a surprising variety of coughs. Most of these signals appear suddenly or develop over a few days to a week.

Circulatory conditions can be trickier to diagnose. Many of the conditions come on slowly, and their symptoms—such as the low-pitched cough of heart disease—may leave you thinking your dog has a cold. Other signs are subtle, including constant fatigue, bluish-tinged tongue and gums, and restlessness. Just how do you learn if your dog has a circulatory condition? Keep a keen eye to any change in your dog's behavior.

Breathing Abnormalities, Including Wheezing and Panting

The purpose of breathing is to provide oxygen for the body and to eliminate the waste gas carbon dioxide. Upon inhalation (also called inspiration), the diaphragm tightens and expands; upon exhalation (also called expiration), it relaxes. Yes, it sounds elementary, but it's important to note, since an absence of this diaphragm movement will result in the cessation of breathing and, consequently, death.

Your pet's normal breathing is worth monitoring. For a dog at rest, a typical breathing rate is between 12 to 20 breaths per minute. (Each time the chest rises for inhalation then relaxes for exhalation is considered 1 breath.) An increase in your pet's normal breathing rate can be caused by pain, high environmental temperature, fever, fear, exercise, or excitement.

None of these fit the mark? An increase in the breathing rate can also signal a respiratory-tract disease, a heart condition, or a metabolic problem. A severe decrease in a dog's breathing rate is commonly associated with shock or a neuromuscular disease.

Often a dog's breathing rate is normal, but the animal has difficulty either inhaling or exhaling. Vets call this **dyspnea,** characterized by noisy breathing or deep, forceful respiratory efforts—or both.

Anatomy could be the cause: Keep in mind that certain breeds—namely flat-faced, short-nosed dogs like pugs, boxers, and bulldogs—are more prone to labored breathing. Noisy breathing is also caused by an anatomical obstruction in the nasal passages, mouth, or larynx as the dog vigorously tries to inhale or exhale (depending on the type of obstruction) against the obstruction. Nonrespiratory conditions that produce exaggerated breathing include elevated body temperature, kidney failure, and diabetes.

Wheezing is considered a specific type of labored breathing, and it sounds just like the wheeze of an asthma-suffering human. It's the result of a lung ailment—such as allergic reactions or bronchitis—that forces a dog's small airways to constrict.

Then there's **panting**, that shallow, rapid breathing characterized by an open mouth and protruding tongue. A dog who has just exercised pants; so does a dog who is feeling too warm due to an overheated room, a rise in body temperature because of stress, or an illness-associated fever.

Panting is appropriate in all these scenarios because it helps your pet cool down. When a dog pants, moisture evaporates from the body, causing the body's temperature to drop slightly.

Panting is nothing to worry about when it follows exercise, time spent in a warm environment, or nervousness. If you can't explain the panting, however, look for additional symptoms that might suggest an underlying illness. Possible related symptoms include fever, coughing, pain, apprehension, or a change in the color of the tongue—all of which should be noted and reported to your vet.

A dog suffering from breathing difficulties—whether changes in rate or in effort—might exhibit other signs as well. The dog may refuse to lie down and may have an anxious expression and/or an open, gaping mouth. The dog may also salivate and/or extend his head and thrust his tongue out. Check your pet's tongue and gums. Do they show a grayish or bluish discoloration? If so, blood oxygen is low. **Take the dog to a vet right away**. Make every attempt to comfort your pet—and thus his breathing.

Breath Accompanied by a Hissing Noise Originating from the Chest

RELATED SYMPTOMS: The hissing noise actually emerges from the chest, not the mouth or nose. The tongue and gums may be tinged a pale blue or gray.

POSSIBLE CAUSE: Can you see an object lodged in your dog's chest or a piece of rib bone breaking the skin? Or is there a puncture wound or gash in the chest area? Your pet may have a **penetrating chest wound** that can create an opening in the chest wall. As air leaks into the chest cavity, the lungs can collapse, making it impossible for the dog to breathe.

CARE: Your goal is to close the wound as quickly as possible. If you have a clean cloth or compress nearby, hold it against the wound. If someone else is available, have that person find an Ace-type wrapping bandage that you can wrap over the compress and around the circumference of the chest and across the shoulders.

Another option is closing the wound with your *clean* fingers. Pinch the tissues together to make an airtight seal. If the respiratory distress is severe and the tongue and gums have turned blue or gray, the blood's oxygen level is low. If a vet is not in close proximity, place a small tube—this can even be the *clean* casing of a pen—into the chest cavity before pinching the tissue closed. To keep the lungs from collapsing, it is important to remove as much air from the chest cavity using whatever suction apparatus you have at hand. A syringe, turkey baster, or your mouth can be used to suck air out of the chest through the tube you have placed in the wound. As soon as the suction has been performed, remove the tube and immediately seal the wound. The dog should be transported to the veterinary hospital as quickly as possible. Acting immediately is necessary to cut the risk of fatal pneumothorax (see the section, Pumping Breathing, p. 88).

PREVENTION: Do not let your dog play outdoors unattended.

Feeble, Shallow Breathing, Accompanied by Panting, Weakness, Stupor, and Pale Mucous Membranes

RELATED SYMPTOMS: The heart rate is rapid and weak, and you may have difficulty finding your pet's pulse. The tongue may be dry and shriveled-looking, the dog may feel unnaturally cold, and he may slip in and out of consciousness.

POSSIBLE CAUSE: Has your dog just experienced some type of medical, physical, or severe psychological trauma? He may be **in shock.** With shock, the blood fails to circulate properly throughout the body. As a result, the tissues and organs do not get enough oxygen to maintain their normal functions. The condition is life-threatening.

CARE: First, address the cause of shock: If the animal is bleeding, apply pressure to slow the flow, then bandage the area. Check the mouth and airway to be sure that they are clear of obstructions. If not, see the Care entry in the section, Vigorous Breathing Efforts, Sometimes Making a Squeaking or Snoring Sound, pp. 91–92. If your pet is not bleeding and nothing is lodged in his throat, wrap him in a warm blanket and immediately take him to the nearest veterinarian's office. The animal is scared. Reduce his stress level with a calm voice and reassuring words. Your vet will treat the dog with oxygen, intravenous fluids, and cortisone.

PREVENTION: To prevent shock from setting in, immediately attend to any emergency or trauma your dog experiences.

Pumping Breathing

RELATED SYMPTOMS: There may also be a shortness of breath with the absence of normal breathing noises, as well as an increased pulse rate and pale blue-tinged or gray-tinged tongue and gums.

POSSIBLE CAUSE: Does your dog play outdoors unsupervised? Was he hit by a car recently? Have your seen him take some type of blow to the chest? Should something hit your pet in his rib cage, small tears may develop in either the skin around the rib cage or the interior lung tissue. Air seeps through these tears into the pleural cavity (the space between the lungs and the chest wall). **Pneumothorax** is the condition's official name, and means **air in the pleural cavity.** The pressure of this errant air not only keeps the lungs from fully expanding, it causes them to collapse. As a result, the dog may suffocate.

CARE: Make sure your dog can breathe freely. Sit him up—perhaps supported by a pillow or rolled-up blankets—**then rush him to the vet.** If the capacity of the lungs is reduced to less than one-third the normal volume, air must be sucked out. Once this is done, the lungs can expand again.

Once home, provide fresh air, quiet, and warmth. Be sure that your dog gets plenty of rest. If a fever develops, antibiotics will be given to ward off infection.

PREVENTION: Keep your pooch leashed when in traffic and don't allow him to play outdoors unsupervised. Perhaps this goes without saying, but never, ever kick or throw an object at your pet's chest. (And don't allow any of the neighborhood kids to either!)

Pumping Breathing with Forced Exhalation and Lack of Appetite

RELATED SYMPTOMS: When exhaling, the abdominal wall is pressed unnaturally inward. There may also be shortness of breath, bluish or gray gums and tongue, vomiting, belching air, and/or weight loss. The dog's abdomen may seem empty, and he may walk slightly hunched. His heartbeat may be muffled or completely inaudible.

POSSIBLE CAUSE: Has your animal recently been hit by a car, bike, ball, or other object? Tears in the diaphragm (also known as a **diaphragmatic hernia**) can result from any strong impact. They can also be present from birth and can go undetected for years. If left unchecked, abdominal organs such as the stomach, intestines, spleen, and liver can migrate into the chest cavity. These traveling organs interfere with breathing and can lead to suffocation.

CARE: Visit your vet. A radiography will determine whether or not a torn diaphragm is the problem. If it is, the same test will show whether stomach organs and intestines have settled in the chest cavity. Surgery can correct diaphragm tears.

PREVENTION: Although you can't thwart defects present from birth, keep your dog away from cars and supervise all outdoor play.

Rapid, Shallow Breathing with Panting

RELATED SYMPTOMS: The breathing may be accompanied by a strong movement of the abdominal wall. The dog may be depressed and lethargic, and may exhibit any or all of the following: a weak, suppressed, painful cough; intermittent fever; periods of restlessness followed by exhaustion; and pumping breathing when the animal sits or stands still.

POSSIBLE CAUSE: Could your dog have come in contact with a sick canine? Have you recently removed a foreign object from his trachea? Or has he experienced a blow to the rib cage? He may be experiencing **pleural effusion**— in lay terms, this means **liquid in the chest.** Prompted by an interior injury or a bacterial, fungal, or viral infection, fluid escapes into the chest cavity. This substance can be blood from injured blood vessels, pus from an infection, or even lymph from a severed lymphatic vessel. This liquid surrounds the lungs and keeps them from expanding, causing the dog to suffocate.

CARE: Take the animal to the vet, who will investigate the cause with X rays, blood tests, or by drawing off a sample of the chest fluid. Specific treatment of pleural effusion is based on the underlying source of the fluid accumulation. Regardless of what prompted the condition, follow-up care will include antibiotics. While he is recuperating, keep your dog relaxed and quiet, and don't allow him to exercise.

PREVENTION: Supervise all outdoor play.

Rattling Breath and Snoring

RELATED SYMPTOMS: There may also be coughing, gagging, empty swallowing, and/or a sudden change in the quality of your dog's bark.

POSSIBLE CAUSE: Has your dog been barking for an extended period of time? Has he had any type of surgical procedure in the last 48 hours that required a breathing tube? It's possible that your pet's larynx is inflamed. Known as **laryngitis**, the condition is rarely anything to worry about.

CARE: Keep your dog rested and away from all bark-inducing stimuli (such as windows where he can see people or other animals) for 48 hours: You want your pet to rest his vocal chords so they can heal. Increasing the humidity in the house can help. You may want to give your dog licorice root (available at your local health-food store), which is a natural cortisone that helps reduce swelling in the throat (see Appendix E, List of Recommended Dosages, pp. 200–223).

Should the animal develop a strained, noisy inhalation during this time, take him to the vet. The larynx could be growing more inflamed and the animal is having difficulty breathing normally.

PREVENTION: You can't avert surgery-induced laryngitis, but you can discourage your dog from barking for extended periods of time.

Vigorous Breathing Efforts, Sometimes Making a Squeaking or Snoring Sound

RELATED SYMPTOMS: The chest wall may not be moving or may actually retract during inhalation. The gums and tongue are tinged a pale blue or gray, and the dog appears to be losing—or has lost—consciousness.

POSSIBLE CAUSE: If your dog has been out of your sight, he could have swallowed or inhaled something that is completely causing an **obstruction of his large, upper airway**.

CARE: Keep your pup cool and avoid aggressive handling which could further stress the dog. If your dog is conscious, perform a modified Heimlich maneuver: Position yourself behind the dog, wrap your arms or hands (depending on the size of the dog) around his abdomen—beneath or behind the rib cage—and briskly squeeze. Try this several times. If it doesn't work, cup your hands and thump the dog's chest several times on both sides.

Do not insert your fingers into your pet's mouth or throat while he is still conscious. This will stress the animal and earn you a nasty bite wound.

Once the animal has lost consciousness, you have 60 to 120 seconds to examine the back of the mouth and throat before the heart stops beating. *Stay calm* and request the help of a second person, if possible. Extend your dog's head and neck forward from his body, open the mouth widely, and pull out the tongue. Visually examine the throat for foreign objects, then explore the area with your fingers. Remove any object you find. If spontaneous breathing does not begin or if there is no heartbeat, perform CPR (see Chapter 1, Breathing: Extremely Difficult or Stopped; Unconsciousness, pp. 7–8). After the ordeal is over, take your pet to the vet for a checkup.

PREVENTION: Remove small knickknacks and other items from your dog's reach.

Wheezing

RELATED SYMPTOM: A wheezing sound typical of a human with severe asthma.

POSSIBLE CAUSE: Has your pet been stung by an insect, confronted with an airborne substance (such as a wall paint or cleaning product), or had an unusually stressful day? Wheezing is usually attributed to narrowing of the larger airways. **Bronchioconstriction**, as the condition is called, is a bit mysterious. Although it's often caused by a type of allergy or an insect sting, it often occurs for absolutely no known reason.

CARE: Whether you suspect an allergic reaction, a bite, or are completely clueless as to the cause, **immediately take your dog to the veterinarian.** Should your vet determine your dog is suffering from bronchioconstriction, she will administer a bronchodilator and/or cortisone injection. If you are unable to get to the vet right away, you may want to administer the following to your dog: vitamin C with bioflavonoids, vitamin B_6, vitamin B_{12}, and an antihistamine such as Chlor-Trimeton (chlorpheniramine) (see Appendix E, List of Recommended Dosages, pp. 200–223).

PREVENTION: In the case of allergy-and insect-caused ailments, keep your dog away from household substances and stinging insects.

Coughing

A dog's cough—just like a human's—is marked by a sudden, noisy expulsion of air from the lungs. Its purpose is a protective one: Coughing is a normal, protective reflex that removes undesired material from the respiratory tract—especially the trachea and large bronchi. This unwelcome material can be an irritant, a piece of food, or phlegm.

Coughs fall into two general categories: nonproductive and productive. A dry, nonproductive cough often sounds harsh or hacking. With a moist, productive cough, the dog may stretch his neck forward and/or lower his head in order to expectorate mucous. You may not see this phlegm, however: Dogs often swallow any secretions they've coughed up.

Coughing in dogs can be confused with other symptoms, specifically gagging, retching, vomiting, regurgitation, wheezing, and reverse sneezing. Coughing expels air; gagging is a throat spasm that prevents matter from traveling down the throat; retching is a stomach spasm that occurs before vomiting; vomiting is a reflex that expels the contents of the stomach (although these, too, may be promptly swallowed); regurgitation is the involuntary, nonpropelled return of undigested food to the mouth after swallowing; wheezing is a type of labored breathing that sounds similar to the noise made by human asthma sufferers; and an episode of reverse sneezing is a spasmotic series of rapid, shallow inhalations through the nose, often resulting from an allergy, sinus condition, or postnasal drip.

Chronic, Honking Cough

RELATED SYMPTOMS: A history of goose-honk coughing in an otherwise healthy small dog. May be accompanied by exercise intolerance, occasional fits of harsher coughing, and full-body collapse during periods of excitement.

POSSIBLE CAUSE: Is your dog a toy or small breed? If so, and nothing else seems wrong, your pet might be suffering from **tracheal collapse.** This can happen in dogs of any age (and occasionally in larger breeds); however, it's most common in petite animals six years and older.

Tracheal collapse is caused by a structural defect that leaves the trachea softer than normal and thus easily collapsed by external pressure (such as a collar), or by internal pressure (such as a sudden intake of air). Moreover, the trachea becomes softer and even more collapsible with age. Although tracheal collapse often occurs by itself, it is also seen in concert with other airway diseases, such as chronic bronchitis.

CARE: If your dog has been coughing for a prolonged period, visit your vet. However, if you are unable to get to the vet's for a while, you can use a human cough suppressant such as Robitussin DM as a temporary treatment (see Appendix E, List of Recommended Dosages, pp. 200–223).

When you go to the vet, he will observe the trachea on an X ray or during an endoscopic examination to differentiate the disorder from other diseases of the airways— including kennel cough, bronchitis, and pneumonia.

Depending on the severity of the condition, surgical correction is an option. This involves implanting support-giving polypropylene rings around the trachea. Cough suppressants and drugs designed to dilate the airways may help relieve symptoms.

PREVENTION: Dogs can live with mildly collapsed tracheas. Indeed, a great many lead near-normal and happy lives. You can't prevent the ailment, but you can take measures to soften the accompanying coughing fits. Minimize daily stress and excitement, since the resulting increased respiratory rate can exacerbate the condition. Switch from a dog collar to a dog harness to minimize pressure on the throat. Also important: *Do not let your dog become overweight.* Excess fat on small dogs often settles in the neck region, further constricting the trachea.

Constant Cough, Possibly Accompanied by Fever, Lethargy, and a Combination of Eye and Nasal Discharge, Diarrhea, Vomiting, and Muscle Spasms

RELATED SYMPTOMS: Besides the foregoing signs, the dog may show no interest in food. These symptoms may become both more serious and more extensive with time and may grow to include breathing difficulties, lowered vision, paralysis, and thickening of the skin on the nosepad and footpads. Several neurologic signs (known collectively as chorea) may also be present, such as circling, rapid eye movements, dementia, involuntary twitching of muscles, and "chewing gum fits" (as the name implies, pets experiencing one of these fits look like they are chewing gum).

POSSIBLE CAUSE: Is your animal young, unvaccinated, or very elderly? Has your pet come in contact with other dogs perhaps on a walk, at the vet's, or at a kennel? If so, he may have **distemper**. A relative of the human measles virus, distemper is a highly infectious viral disease that also goes by the name of **canine distemper, CDV,** and **Carré's disease**. It is transmitted by airborne moisture droplets and by contact with infected urine and fecal matter.

CARE: Take your pet immediately to the veterinarian. To determine if the condition is distemper and not kennel cough (which it approximates early on) or rabies (which it resembles later on), your vet will ask for a history of the dog's exposure to other animals, note symptoms, and look into the absence of proper vaccinations. In addition, direct microscopic evidence of the virus within blood cells or conjunctival scrapings of the eye can help your vet make a diagnosis.

If you are unable to bring the dog to the vet for a few days, try giving him high doses of vitamin C every 2 to 3 hours during the day. If diarrhea occurs, it may be caused by the disease or the vitamin C: Try stopping the vitamin C for 1 day, and if the diarrhea improves, lower the dose of vitamin C. (See Appendix E, List of Recommended Dosages, pp. 200–223).

No cure for canine distemper currently exists. Although distemper itself may not kill a dog, the secondary complications it causes can be fatal. Therefore, treatment is aimed at preventing the secondary complications: using antibiotics for bacterial infections; fluid replacement to right the effects of diarrhea, vomiting, and appetite loss; antidiarrhea medications to regulate elimination; and anticonvulsive therapies should seizures occur. Since the illness is so very infectious, many vets will not hospitalize ailing dogs; they don't want to infect other animals. Thus, it may be left to you to administer your pet's medication.

During this time, your pup must be strictly quarantined to squelch the spread of distemper to other dogs and area animals (this includes ferrets, foxes, wolves, coyotes, weasels, skunks, badgers, and raccoons). To inactivate any virus microbes that have settled in the home, disinfect all hard surfaces with a solution of 1 part bleach to 30 parts water.

PREVENTION: Canine distemper is a frightening disease. It's also easily preventable with inoculation. Between the ages of 6 and 16 weeks, have your pet vaccinated every 2 or 3 weeks. During this time period, keep your dog away from unknown animals and avoid parks or other areas frequented by large numbers of unsupervised canines. While at your vet's office, hold your puppy in your lap to avoid contact with possible sick animals. Dogs often lose their immunity as they grow older, so annual booster CDV vaccinations are wise. Checking the dog's level of antibody protection against distemper could be performed yearly. If antibody protection is high, then annual vaccine may not be needed.

Coughing, Accompanied by a Swollen Abdomen and Loose Stools

RELATED SYMPTOMS: Your pet may have no appetite, may be weak, and may look as if he has lost weight, in spite of his swollen abdomen.

POSSIBLE CAUSE: Is your pet a puppy or an older dog who you recently brought home from a pound, pet store, or breeder? There's a chance he is infested with **roundworms,** internal parasites that live in the intestines. They are transmitted by eggs found in the feces of infected dogs, or by rodents who have been infected. Roundworms will cause the pup to be unhealthy-looking and underweight even though the distended abdomen may give him the appearance of being fat.

CARE: See your vet, who will examine your pet's stool for the presence of roundworm eggs. If your dog is playing host to the parasite, your vet will deworm the animal or give you medication that is given to the dog for several days then repeated several weeks later.

PREVENTION: Take all new pets to the vet for routine deworming. Stool samples should be checked 3 to 4 times a year. Keep your dog away from the stools of other dogs.

Deep, Racking Cough, Accompanied by Weight Loss, Lethargy, Bouts of Fever, and Labored Breathing

RELATED SYMPTOMS: There will be a loss of appetite, and you may or may not notice enlarged lymph nodes, appetite loss, retching, vomiting, diarrhea, and jaundice.

POSSIBLE CAUSE: Has your pet been near a sick, coughing, sneezing human? If the dog is an urban one, has he been in close proximity to a street person? There's a possibility he could have **tuberculosis**. A very rare condition, **TB** (as it's also called) is spread by the respiratory secretions, usually those of infected persons when they cough or sneeze. The bacteria that causes tuberculosis can attack all organs, though it most often locates in the lungs and intestines.

CARE: The symptoms of tuberculosis can be nearly identical to respiratory illnesses such as pneumonia, bronchitis, and kennel cough. If, after 48 hours of restful quarantine—in a warm part of the house—the symptoms have not disappeared, visit your vet. She will perform a biopsy of lymph-node tissue and a bacterial culture. Local public-health authorities should be notified immediately if your dog is diagnosed with the illness.

Treatment is long: Sometimes it takes more than 1 year's worth of antituberculosis medication to heal an infected dog. Animals undergoing treatment represent a potential disease threat to all people and animals they come in contact with. If your pet has been diagnosed with TB, all human and animal members of the household must undergo medical examination.

PREVENTION: There is no canine vaccination against TB. The best preventative measure is to keep the animal away from suspected human carriers.

Dry Cough, Accompanied by Breathing Difficulties and Exercise Intolerance

RELATED SYMPTOMS: The cough may or may not produce blood. Fainting spells, rapid breathing, increased pulse rate, lethargy, weight loss, loss of stamina, and a swollen belly due to fluid buildup in the abdomen may also be present.

POSSIBLE CAUSE: Are mosquitoes prevalent in your locale? Does your dog spend time outside? Have you been lax in giving your dog heartworm-preventive medicine? If so, there's a chance he may have **heartworm disease**. The heartworm parasite is spread by the mosquito, which bites your dog, simultaneously passing its larvae into your pet's bloodstream. Once there, the larvae migrate to the heart, make a home for themselves, and grow into adult worms. In turn, these adult worms send their larvae into the bloodstream for another mosquito to suck up and deposit into yet another dog. The worms themselves are long, threadlike things (often 14 inches) with small mouths. If not treated, they can live lodged in your dog for 5 years (which is the average lifespan of a heartworm).

By the time the worms have lived in your dog for 6 months, they are fully mature. An inflammatory response to the parasites may develop and your pet's pulmonary arteries may become enlarged. As these worms die, they can lodge themselves in a blood vessel of the lung, blocking it and stressing the heart to the point where some dogs die of heart attacks or pneumonia.

CARE: If your dog is fainting or coughing, **take him to the vet immediately**. Keep the dog extremely quiet (i.e., cage rest is advisable, with absolutely no exercise).

To determine what ails the animal, your vet will give him a thorough exam to rule out other respiratory illnesses such as kennel cough and distemper. This checkup will feature a blood test to detect both the presence of the heartworms' larvae and the specific proteins that the adult worms shed into the bloodstream. Blood testing should always be performed before heartworm medication is administered. Some vets may also choose to perform a chest X ray to look for the enlarged pulmonary arteries indicative of heartworm infestation.

Ridding the body of worms requires an arsenical compound administered intravenously 2 times a day for 2 days. A 2- to 7-day hospital stay is commonly recommended. Worms begin dying 5 to 10 days after therapy. During this time, strictly confine your pet indoors and keep exercise or excitement in check. Both of these can increase blood flow in the pulmonary arteries, upping the odds that a large mass of worms will be carried into the lungs. (This can block the pulmonary blood flow and cause a severe reaction, including cough, fever, and pneumonia. Such reactions must be treated immediately with antibiotics and corticosteroids.) The goal is for dead worms to gradually pass into the lungs, where your pet's immune defenses eliminate them.

Anywhere from 4 to 6 weeks after the adult worms have been treated, a second medication is administered to kill any larvae still swimming in the bloodstream.

PREVENTION: Because some dogs with heartworm show no apparent signs, have your pet's blood tested every 6 months if you live in a mosquito-friendly, heartworm-prevalent area and keep your dog inside during mosquito-active times. If your locale is only sparsely populated with mosquitos, a once-yearly checkup is still a good idea. Antiheartworm drugs are available and are highly recommended in mosquito-infested areas.

Dry, Harsh, Crouplike, Episodic Cough, Possibly Accompanied by Frothy Mucous and Gagging Fits

RELATED SYMPTOMS: Sudden bouts of loud, forceful, hacking coughs—especially after exercise or drinking—in an otherwise bright, healthy dog. These episodes are often followed by drawn-out retching or gagging motions that sometimes produce a foamy mucous. There may also be small amounts of foamy mucous at the corners of the mouth and that coat the back of the throat. Though the throat and tonsils may be reddened and inflamed, the dog's appetite remains hearty.

POSSIBLE CAUSE: Does your pooch pal around with neighborhood dogs? Have you and your pet come across a sick dog on a walk? Was your pet boarded recently? Is he a show animal? Does your dog bark excessively, especially when confined? If the answer to any of these questions is "yes," **kennel cough** may be the culprit. Kennel cough is actually the common name given to an entire group of respiratory diseases—all with identical symptoms—that infect the cells lining the windpipe and bronchial airways.

Kennel cough, also known by its medical name, **infectious tracheobronchitis**, is highly contagious. It's transmitted by infected moisture droplets that are expelled into the air by an afflicted canine's coughs. If one of these droplets finds its way into the eyes, nose, or mouth of your pet—either directly or by landing on a surface that your dog then licks—your pet can become infected.

CARE: No matter how mild the cough, if your dog is younger than five months or older than three years, have your vet give the animal a physical examination so you can be sure a more serious problem does not exist. Otherwise, a mild case of kennel cough in a healthy dog can heal in about 2 or 3 weeks without treatment. Yet, just as a human cold can worsen into pneumonia, kennel cough also has the potential to deteriorate into pneumonia. Thus it's important to keep the animal quarantined—you don't want other dogs getting sick! In its early stages, kennel cough can be hard to distinguish from distemper.

If you cannot get to the vet right away, you can give your dog a human cough suppressant such as Robitussin DM to temporarily relieve coughing (see Appendix E, List of Recommended Dosages, pp. 200–223). Your objective is to keep the dog as well rested as possible. Avoid any stressful, cough-inducing circumstances—such as inviting people into your home whom your pet doesn't know or walking him on a leash. Be sure to take your dog's temperature daily if you decide to rely on home treatment: 101.5°F is a normal temperature for most dogs.

If a fever develops, the dog becomes less active, his appetite decreases, a greenish discharge appears at the eyes or nose, or the animal has difficulty breathing, take care! Pneumonia may have set in. **See your vet immediately**.

As mentioned, kennel cough can resemble canine distemper. Which is why after noting the dog's symptoms and requesting a history of your pet's exposure to other canines, your vet may perform radiography to determine the condition of the lungs and airway. Viral studies and bacterial cultures may also be taken.

Once diagnosed, your vet will outline a course of action to reduce coughing and ward off pneumonia, reduce fever, and prevent dehydration. To head off complications involving the lungs, antibiotics are often given. Your vet might also prescribe a decongestant to reduce the flow of mucous. Or, a vaporizer may be suggested to liquefy the phlegm that has built up in your dog's airway. It sounds unpleasant, but this liquefied mucous is easier for the dog to expel through his mouth and nose than stickier, more viscous secretions. If you don't have access to a vaporizer, your vet might suggest placing the dog in a steam-filled bathroom for 10 to 15 minutes, or letting him lie on the bathroom rug while you take your shower. Carefully monitor the temperature and provide plenty of drinking water—you don't want your dog to become dehydrated or overheated!

If constant coughing has left your pet exhausted, a cough suppressant may be administered. Usually, though, coughing is encouraged to clear secretions from the airways. A word of warning: Cough suppressant or no cough suppressant, even after kennel cough has been successfully treated, coughing can continue for up to 3 weeks.

PREVENTION: Will your dog be spending a significant

amount of time at kennels, grooming parlors, or dog shows? Look into the *Bordetella bronchiseptica* vaccine. It can be given to pups as young as six weeks, with recommended annual revaccination. This particular vaccine is also available as nosedrops and through injection. These vaccines generate local immunity in the upper-respiratory tract, which also happens to be kennel cough's path of entry.

Other helpful vaccines include the parainfluenza virus vaccine. You may remember this one. It's typically given in serial doses: the first when a puppy is 6 to 8 weeks old, then every 3 to 4 weeks thereafter until the pup reaches 14 to 18 weeks. Annual revaccination then follows. (If a pet owner doesn't want to vaccinate yearly, serum titer tests are available that measure the dog's level of immunity, hence a dog with a high titer does not need to be revaccinated.)

Long Fits of Wet Cough, Accompanied by Whistling Noises

RELATED SYMPTOMS: The cough will be deep and exhaling difficulties may also be present.

POSSIBLE CAUSE: Has your dog been exposed to harmful, irritating environmental substances? Did he inhale foreign matter (wood chips, pollen, sand, dust, etc.) days earlier that could possibly be stuck in the lungs? If so, it's possible that he has **allergic** or **foreign body bronchitis**.

Older dogs, especially smaller breeds such as poodles, beagles, and terriers, can develop chronic bronchitis. Despite the coughing, most dogs with allergic bronchitis are otherwise healthy, although they may be unable to exercise for long periods of time without becoming fatigued.

CARE: If fever is present, **immediately take the dog to the vet**. In the absence of high temperature, you can try homecare for 48 hours. (See the entry Care in the section, Dry, Harsh, Crouplike, Episodic Cough, Possibly Accompanied by Frothy Mucous and Gagging Fits, p. 99.) You may also want to give your dog Benadryl, which acts as an antihistamine and sedative and will help to keep the animal quiet and calm, or a human cough suppressant like Robitussin DM. Supplementing your dog's diet with vitamin A, vitamin C (a natural antihistamine), and sulfur will reduce respiratory-tract inflammation. (see Appendix E, List of Recommended Dosages, pp. 200–223). If symptoms have not improved after 2 days, visit the vet.

Your vet will attempt to establish the cause of the allergy by taking an extensive history or possibly using a RAST test. Once the offending substance is discovered, it should be removed from the dog's environment if possible—for example, discontinuing use or changing brands of deodorizers, flea sprays, perfumes, etc. If the substance cannot be removed, such as in the case of plant pollens or molds, anti-inflammatory or anti-allergy medication may be prescribed. Because many ailments (from heart failure to cancer) can produce coughing, X rays and an endoscopic examination are often performed. When coughing is continual, cough suppressants may be considered. Severe allergic bronchitis is most effectively controlled with long-term, low doses of oral anti-inflammatory medication. Your vet may also prescribe a bronchodilator, a drug that causes the airways to expand, allowing for improved respiration.

PREVENTION: As it does in people, dry air can aggravate a dog's tendency to develop bronchitis. A comfortable humidity level is 50 to 60 percent. (A humidifier can help make your environment less arid.)

Low-Pitched Cough More Common in Morning, at Night, and with Exertion

RELATED SYMPTOMS: This deep cough may also occur when your pet drinks, exercises, or becomes excited. Accompanying it may be any combination of the following: mucous, bubbly white sputum, weakness, fainting, rapid heart rate, bluish-colored tongue and gums, restlessness, inability to exercise without tiring or weakening quickly, and a swollen abdomen. Your dog might stand with his front legs spread wide apart and his neck extended downward in an effort to breathe, and he may develop a penchant for resting in cool, well-ventilated spots. You may have noticed that these symptoms have grown worse with time.

POSSIBLE CAUSE: Is yours a mature dog? Or is he a Doberman, boxer, Great Dane, Irish wolfhound, Saint Bernard, golden retriever or German shepherd? Is he a small breed, such as cavalier King Charles spaniel, Chihuahua, or fox terrier? If so, he may have a **heart condition**—either congenital or acquired. Whether the cause is due to genes, age, or infection, a heart condition often prompts an enlarged heart and fluid buildup in the lungs, which in turn prompts coughing.

The term **heart disease** covers many specific conditions: valve-related ailments, illnesses involving the heart muscle itself, and congenital narrowing of the pulmonary artery and aorta—all of which usually force the heart to become progressively less efficient at pumping blood, until the organ can no longer supply the body's needs, a condition known as heart failure. (Many people think heart failure means the heart has stopped beating; in actuality it means the heart is failing to pump blood adequately, causing pulmonary (lung) congestion and heart enlargement to occur.) Yet, heart disease doesn't have to lead to sudden death: Many types can be present long before actual failure occurs. In fact, heart disease generally progresses through several treatable stages before heart failure takes place.

CARE: Isolate your pooch for 48 hours, taking pains not to allow him to become excited, overly active, or too hot or cold. If the condition has not changed in this time span, visit the vet.

To determine if your pet has a heart condition, your vet will listen to the organ (a murmur caused by irregular blood flow through the diseased heart is a giveaway) feel for the pulse, take X rays, and possibly perform an electrocardiogram (ECG).

Treatment involves improving circulatory function. Your vet will probably place your pet on a low-sodium diet to prevent fluid retention. If needed, she will recommend medication to dilate the airways, drugs to increase the strength of heart contractions, blood-pressure medicine to dilate vessels, and diuretics to help control the sodium and water retention that accompanies heart failure. If an infection of the valves or lining of the heart is causing heart failure, antibiotics will be prescribed.

There are additional things you can do at home to strengthen your dog's heart. Hawthorne berry (available at health-food stores) is an herb frequently used for heart problems that strengthens and repairs heart muscle and can be used on a long-term basis. To find the correct dosage for your pet, give him 3 drops 3 times a day for 5 days, then increase the dose by 1 drop and repeat the schedule for another 5 days. Continue this until the dog's cardiac cough begins to subside and he appears more energetic. Dandelion and parsley are herbal diuretics, which can help to reduce pulmonary congestion.

Vitamin and mineral supplements can also be useful in strengthening the heart. Add the following to your dog's diet: vitamin E, vitamin A, zinc, and vitamin C (see Appendix E, List of Recommended Dosages, pp. 200–223).

PREVENTION: Most types of heart disease cannot be prevented, although the same preventative measures that apply to humans apply to dogs: Obesity should be avoided! Special diets and nutrients are available to support the heart's function.

Persistent Dry Cough

RELATED SYMPTOMS: The cough is usually mild, but it is constant. Breathing difficulties and retching may also be present.

POSSIBLE CAUSES: Has your pet eaten or licked another dog's feces? He may be infected with several species of **parasitic worms**, such as **roundworms** or **hookworms**. Once your dog ingests the eggs of these worms, the eggs travel into the intestinal tract, where they grow into larvae. They then penetrate the intestinal wall and migrate into the lungs, where they irritate the bronchial passages. The larvae are eventually coughed up into the dog's mouth and swallowed back into the intestinal tract, where they finally mature into adult worms. The adult worms live and thrive in the intestinal tract and produce more eggs, which then exit the body via the feces. (There are also a number of other parasitic worms, such as lungworms and heartworms, which live primarily in the lungs and can also cause persistent coughs. For more information on heartworms, see section, Dry Cough, Accompanied by Breathing Difficulties and Exercise Intolerance, pp. 98–99; for information specifically on roundworms, see section, Coughing, Accompanied by a Swollen Abdomen and Loose Stools, pp. 96–97.)

CARE: This is one of those usually-not-health-threatening conditions that, nevertheless, requires a veterinarian's care. Because eggs are passed in the stool, your vet will need to examine your dog's feces. To kill the eggs, a vet will give your dog a dewormer.

Wormwood and garlic are touted by many to be natural worm remedies, however, I have also treated many worm infestations where garlic and/or wormwood have failed to work. Because roundworms and hookworms can be directly or indirectly transmitted to humans, I recommend working closely with your veterinarian rather than opting to use over-the-counter remedies.

PREVENTION: Watch what goes into your dog's mouth— and what his tongue touches. If you want to aid your dog in fending off the invading parasites, upgrade his diet with a chemical-free, high-quality diet, supplemented with digestive-enzyme supplements and antioxidant vitamins C and E (see Appendix E, List of Recommended Dosages, pp. 200–223). These help the body's immune system deal with the parasitic invaders.

Single Episode of Dry Coughing

RELATED SYMPTOM: Hacking-sounding cough that produces no mucous or blood and is not accompanied by fever or swollen glands.

POSSIBLE CAUSE: Has the animal recently been fed? Has he been rooting in dirt? Underfoot during housecleaning? If the cough appears directly after any of these activities, there's a chance **something went down the wrong pipe**. Yes, it happens to animals too: Instead of gliding down the esophagus to the stomach, a bit of food or liquid—even dust, dirt, a toy, or a household cleanser—travels down the windpipe, which leads to the lungs. Coughing forces the object out of the airway back into the throat where it can make its way down the correct passageway— or be spit out.

CARE: Observe the dog. He should cough freely for a minute, then stop once the windpipe has been cleared. If the coughing continues and/or is accompanied by a refusal to eat, restlessness, blood, and/or excess saliva, a piece of food or other foreign object may have become lodged in the animal's throat or windpipe. Contact your veterinarian. (If coughing persists for more than 5 minutes without stopping or the dog is in very serious trouble, consider performing the Heimlich maneuver. Position yourself behind the dog, wrap your arms or hands (depending on the size of the dog) around his abdomen—beneath or behind the rib cage—and briskly squeeze. Try this several times. If it doesn't work, cup your hands and thump the dog's chest several times on both sides.

Do not insert your fingers into your pet's mouth or throat while he is still conscious. This will stress the animal and earn you a nasty bite wound.

Once the animal has lost consciousness, you have 60 to 120 seconds to examine the back of the mouth and throat before the heart stops beating. *Stay calm* and request the help of a second person, if possible. Extend your dog's head and neck forward from his body, open the mouth widely, and pull out the tongue. Visually examine the throat for foreign objects, then explore the area with your fingers. Remove any object you find. After the ordeal is over, take your pet to the vet for a checkup. If the dog passes out, look down his throat for a foreign object that you could remove by yourself.

Once at the vet's, she will determine the nature of the

obstruction, performing a radiographic or endoscopic examination in an attempt to view the object. The object is usually extracted from the throat with a probe or endoscope while the dog is under anesthesia. Should the object be lodged in the esophagus rather than the windpipe, your vet may simply push it into the stomach. If an infection has set in, the animal will be put on a soft-food diet for 1 to 2 weeks and given antibiotics.

PREVENTION: Never give your pet large bones, such as vertebrae, to gnaw on. Furthermore, ban all small balls and sharp toys, and place your dog in another room when cleaning, thus limiting his contact with dust and cleaning products.

Wet Cough, Accompanied by Depression and Fever

RELATED SYMPTOMS: The cough will be weak and perhaps painful—it can also be artificially triggered by tapping your pet's chest. In addition, your dog may have nasal and eye discharge, weight loss, lethargy, and labored breathing with shorter, more rapid breaths than usual.

POSSIBLE CAUSE: Has your dog recently had bronchitis, kennel cough, or distemper? Has he undergone surgery for laryngeal paralysis or been anesthetized (both of which can lead to accidental inhalation of material from the mouth into the lungs)? Has your pet been exposed to noxious fumes within the past 24 to 48 hours? Any of these can lead to **pneumonia**, an inflammatory condition of the lung. Any animal can get pneumonia, but it most often strikes those under two years of age and older than eight years.

CARE: If 48 hours of homecare—including abundant rest in a warm room with 50 to 60 percent humidity and lots of fluids—hasn't eradicated the symptoms, take your pet to the vet. Quite a few illnesses share symptoms with pneumonia, which is why your vet will take chest X rays to help reach a diagnosis. To determine the underlying cause of the pneumonia, samples of lung secretions are obtained for microscopic examination and for bacterial and fungal culture. This is done using either local or general anesthesia.

Treatment includes intravenous or subcutaneous (beneath the skin) fluid administration, maintenance of normal body temperature, rest, and perhaps antibiotics and expectorants. (See the Care entry in the section, Dry, Harsh, Crouplike, Episodic Cough, Possibly Accompanied by Frothy Mucous and Gagging Fits, pp. 99–101.) Coax your pet to gently walk around the house a few times daily. This stimulates the cough reflex, which can help break up mucous. Depending on what is causing the pneumonia, specific antibiotics or antifungal drugs may be prescribed. You can also help to strengthen your dog's immune system by giving him vitamins C and A (see Appendix E, List of Recommended Dosages, pp. 200–223).

PREVENTION: Because many respiratory conditions can worsen into pneumonia, the best prevention is to immediately treat these conditions.

Sneezing

Sneezing is not an illness. It's a sign that some type of condition exists—usually a problem in the nasal passages or sinuses. A canine sneeze is really no different from a human's: A forceful expulsion of air travels through the airways at great speed. In both person and pup, the sneeze is a reflex—ordinarily brought about by an irritation in the mucous membranes lining the nasal cavity—that helps clear the respiratory passages. Sneezing more commonly accompanies a suddenly occurring condition rather than a chronic disorder.

Chronic Sneezing, Noisy Breathing, and Foul-Smelling, Watery Nasal Discharge

RELATED SYMPTOMS: The dog frequently paws at or rubs his face. Any combination of the following may also be present: bloody nasal discharge, reverse sneezing, puss and scabs on the sides of the nose, and plugged nostrils.

POSSIBLE CAUSE: It is possible your dog has **rhinitis**—

which in vet-speak means a **canine head cold** complete with inflamed nasal passages. This can be caused by a virus, a bacterial infection, or even an airborne allergen. In some dogs—like some humans who have habitual colds—it can be chronic.

CARE: If it becomes chronic, rhinitis can destroy nasal cartilage. If you suspect it, be safe rather than sorry and take your pet to the vet. She will take a sample of the nasal discharge. If the diagnosis is, indeed, rhinitis, your vet will clean your dog's nostrils—allowing for easier breathing. Depending on what is causing the ailment, antibiotics, corticosteroids, and/or antihistamines will be given.

In the event that you are unable to reach the vet for a few days, you can try giving your dog an oral antihistamine like chlorpheniramine (Chlor-Trimeton) (see Appendix E, List of Recommended Dosages, pp. 200–223) to dry up his runny nose. Cleaning your dog's nasal passages carefully with a Q-Tip to clear away any mucous can help him to breathe easier and make him more comfortable.

PREVENTION: Keep any nasal condition from getting worse by keeping your dog's nose clean and obtaining good veterinary advice.

Reverse Sneezing

At some point you may have heard a loud, spasmatic snorting noise burst from your pet's nose. Called a reverse sneeze, the sound is very dramatic—and frightening. Fortunately, reverse sneeze attacks are sporadic. More good news: Reverse sneezing ordinarily occurs in dogs who are otherwise healthy and is brought on by something relatively harmless: typically an allergy, water drinking, excitement, postnasal drip, or pressure from a collar. What you're hearing is your pet trying to clear the back of his nasal passages. This usually takes from 10 second to 2 minutes.

It is theorized that dogs with sensitive throats—due to irritation caused by an incomplete opening of the **epiglottis** after swallowing—are those most likely to reverse sneeze. Usually no treatment is needed.

A reverse sneeze is a startling, "here one minute, gone the next" kind of thing and should not be confused with the snoring or squeaking that animals with partial large-airway obstructions may make when trying to breathe.

If your pet suffers from attacks of reverse sneezing several times a day or for more than 30 seconds on a regular basis, talk to your veterinarian to be sure the noise is indeed a reverse sneeze.

If so, your vet may prescribe medicine that will reduce the occurence of this benign but upsetting behavior. If she finds that the noise is caused by an elongated soft palate that impinges on the epiglottis, she may recommend the removal of a portion of the dog's soft palate.

CHAPTER 8

Abdomen

When vets talk about your dog's abdomen, they aren't just referring to the stomach. The abdomen is a large, hollow cavity filled with various organs. The stomach is one of these organs, but also included are the kidneys, liver, bladder, intestines, and reproductive organs. A problem with any of these can manifest itself as a tummyache or with bloating, bleeding, a change in elimination habits, lethargy, bad breath, and a variety of other subtle-to-showy signals. A problem with the abdominal wall itself, like a tear in its tissue or a hernia, also may show a variety of seemingly unrelated symptoms.

Because illnesses involving the internal organs can be serious—or even fatal—keep an eye out for any behavioral changes or a barely perceptible deviation in your pet's health.

Bloated, Distended, or Painful Abdomen

A belly can become swollen for any number of reasons. There are the obvious ones: Your dog has just eaten a big meal, taken in excess carbohydrates or protein (table scraps maybe?), or drunk a large volume of water. Excess gas production also may cause her stomach to become distended.

Causes that are harder to pinpoint lead to slow, gradual abdominal distension, perhaps over 1 day's or 1 week's time. Conditions that commonly cause this condition include **constipation** or **abdominal fluid retention** (called **ascites**) caused by **kidney failure, liver disease**, a **hor-**

monal imbalance (such as **Cushing's disease**), **abdominal tumors**, or **organ enlargements**.

Because a number of different illnesses can cause a distended abdomen, your vet will narrow the diagnostic field by viewing a swollen abdomen in light of any accompanying symptoms, such as vomiting, restlessness, or a change in elimination habits.

As for stomach pain, you'll know your pet's abdomen hurts if she shrinks from being touched there, moves cautiously or not at all, and adopts either an arched-back stance or what vets call a prayer pose (back legs standing, front legs outstretched and lowered onto the ground, head resting on front legs). A dog with a stomachache might refuse food, tremble, and/or cry. A tender tummy most commonly indicates an injury or disease of one of the organs housed in the abdomen.

Bloated Abdomen, Vomiting, Excess Salivation, and Rapid Breathing

RELATED SYMPTOMS: Restlessness and/or weakness may also be present.

POSSIBLE CAUSE: Did your dog recently eat a large meal and/or drink a large volume of water, then exercise or roll onto her back? She could have **GDV**, also known as **gastric dilation-volvulus complex** or **gastric torsion**. Although the ailment can strike any dog, deep-chested breeds such as boxers, sheepdogs, setters, standard poodles, Great Danes, and Saint Bernards are especially susceptible.

Three things team up to cause GDV: One is a short supply of gastric acid, which is needed to digest a large meal, the second is physical activity, and the third is excessive food and water consumption. This situation generates gas that bloats the not-yet-emptied stomach. To make an unpleasant situation even more uncomfortable, gas continues to form as the undigested food ferments. This bloating twists the filled-to-capacity stomach into an unnatural position, blocking the exit for the stomach's contents—

meaning the food and gas have no escape. This coiling also crimps blood vessels, which interrupts the gastric blood supply.

CARE: Take your dog immediately to the vet, who will study her symptoms and medical history to reach a diagnosis. Providing the belly isn't too twisted, your vet will insert a tube down the esophagus into the stomach in order to siphon out some of the contents and relieve the gas distention. If this is impossible, surgery will be performed to untwist the stomach and relieve the bloat. Your pet may be given intravenous fluids, steroids, and/or antibiotics to prevent shock from setting in.

PREVENTION: Give your pooch smaller, more frequent feedings and don't let her exercise vigorously or roll on her back for 1 hour after eating or drinking heavily. Should your dog have a predisposition toward repeated episodes of GDV, your vet might stitch the stomach to the abdominal wall to prevent it from twisting.

Obvious Bulge At Midabdomen, Groin, or Rectal Area

RELATED SYMPTOM: The dog may appear restless.

POSSIBLE CAUSES: Has your dog been in an accident lately? Has she recently overexerted herself physically? Is she a pregnant female or a new mother? Is he an older male who has been diagnosed with an enlarged prostate and is frequently constipated? Your pet may have one of several types of hernia, including an **umbilical hernia** (at the navel), an **inguinal hernia** (of the groin), or a **perineal hernia** (of the genital region). Standing the animal on her hind legs makes it easier to see the hernia bulge out.

Hernias happen when interior muscles tear after being suddenly strained beyond their capacity. These muscles act as a kind of containing wall to hold organs in place. A rip in this muscular wall allows organs or fat to "poke through" the injury and situate themselves directly beneath the skin— these runaway tissues comprise the hernia's visible surface bulge. Depending on the type and size of the hernia, the dog may feel little or a great deal of discomfort. Hernias can be life-threatening if a loop of intestine passes into the hernia and becomes twisted, losing the blood supply.

CARE: Visit the vet, who can usually diagnose the problem with a physical exam. If your dog does have a hernia, your vet may perform an operation to repair it.

PREVENTION: Although hernias are difficult to prevent, the sooner the problem is recognized and addressed, the less discomfort and health risks your pooch suffers.

Change in Appetite and/or Weight

No one wants to read a lecture about the perils of letting a dog get fat. Yet, obesity is the number-one canine health disorder seen in veterinarian's offices. Statistics vary, but according to studies from the School of Veterinary Medicine, University of California at Davis, 25 to 44 percent of all dogs are overweight (compare that with 6 to 12 percent of cats). A pooch weighing over 15 percent more than the standard accepted weight for her height is considered obese. Just how serious is this extra body fat? A portly pooch is at increased risk for **musculoskeletal, cardiovascular, gastrointestinal, endocrine, respiratory, immune,** and **reproductive disorders,** including **cancer.**

Common, nonmedical factors contributing to a canine's growing girth are predictable ones: high-fat diets (many of the so-called premium brands of dog food are high in fat), eating too much (when given the opportunity, dogs happily eat more than their bodies need), lack of adequate exercise (one daily stroll around the block isn't enough), and being fed little dog treats throughout the day. Correct one or more of these situations and an overweight pooch will usually begin to slim down.

Instances occur, however, when obesity can only be blamed on a medical condition that increases a dog's appetite, putting her in a continual state of ravenousness. In veterinary terms, the act of eating more than normal is called **polyphagia,** typically caused by illnesses involving a hormonal imbalance. The affected dog eats dinner, continues to act hungry, and is given more food by her attentive owner. Unfortunately, after a few months of this, the dog begins to get pudgy.

But what if you monitor your pet's diet, wouldn't dream of feeding her table scraps, give her plenty of exercise, and notice her growing fat anyway? You'd probably worry that something was wrong—and rightly so. Changes in food intake and/or weight are good indicators that your dog might be ailing. In the foregoing example, a slower metabolism due to age, illness, or an increasingly sedentary lifestyle is a strong possibility: A dog who isn't burning calories is going to store them as fat.

What about the pooch whose diet and lifestyle haven't changed (meaning she's not consuming less calories or burning more) but who is still losing weight? One explanation is that the dog isn't assimilating the calories and nutrients she is taking in, a common occurrence in **diabetes**. You may even notice the dog becoming weak, lethargic, or apathetic. **Diseases of the intestinal lining** can result in poor absorption of nutrients.

Of course, the most obvious road to weight loss is via appetite loss. Vets call this **anorexia.** Unlike the psychologically based human illness of the same name, the condition in dogs is a physical one that accompanies a wide range of medical conditions—from internal infection to cancer or other diseases of one of the abdominal organs. Internal parasites, such as tapeworms or hookworms, can steal nutrition from the animal, resulting in chronic weight loss. Simply put, an animal who doesn't feel well often can't stomach the thought of food. And without her regular calorie supply, she loses weight.

Weight Loss in Spite of Voracious Appetite, Accompanied by Excessive Thirst and Urination, Listlessness, and Lethargy

RELATED SYMPTOMS: The coat may appear dull and the dog may scratch it occasionally. The animal may de-

velop a potbelly and bad breath that smells faintly of ace-
tone.

POSSIBLE CAUSE: Is yours an older animal? Is she overweight? Is she a midsized dog? She may have **diabetes,** an
illness (just like the human version) that originates with
inadequate insulin production. The pancreas is responsible
for manufacturing insulin, a substance that regulates the
metabolism of sugar in the blood. Without sufficient insulin, blood sugar rises but remains in the bloodstream, unable to get to the body's cells, where it is desperately
needed. The body may utilize its fat in place of sugar in
order to supply itself with energy. This imbalance leads to
kidney, liver, eye, and heart failure and, eventually, death.

CARE: It's possible to determine whether your dog has
excess blood sugar with an at-home urine test available at
your pharmacy (you can buy the same test used for humans). Keep in mind that normal urine does not contain
sugar. Whether you try a home test or not (and regardless
of the outcome), you will still need to visit the vet for a
formal diagnosis, which will hinge on a blood sample.
Should your dog have diabetes, she will be placed on insulin therapy.

At the beginning of therapy, the dog usually stays under
close veterinary supervision for the first 2 or 3 days while
the correct insulin dose is determined. From then on, however, you will be responsible for giving your pet daily injections, feeding her a strict high-fiber/low-fat diet doled
out in 4 small meals, and providing round-the-clock access
to drinking water. Your vet may ask you to test your
pooch's urine regularly (using the at-home strip method).
Should you discover sugar in her urine, the necessary insulin adjustments can be made immediately.

You can also supplement your dog's diet with zinc,
chromium, and a standard antioxidant vitamin-mineral supplement. A high-quality digestive-enzyme supplement that
is high in lipase should be given to your dog regularly (see
Appendix E, List of Recommended Dosages, pp. 200–223).

PREVENTION: Feed your dog a high-fiber, low-fat diet

that is free of simple sugars and chemicals. Don't let her become overweight.

Change in Thirst and Irregular Urination

A constant supply of fresh water is important for dogs to keep dehydration at bay. But there may come a time when you notice your dog dipping into the water bowl more and more frequently—or infrequently. When not accompanied by other symptoms, a one-or two-day change in drinking habits is usually not cause for alarm. Maybe the weather is hot or your pet has depleted her body's water levels with more-vigorous-than-usual play.

If the thirst pattern continues, there could be a problem. **Kidney and liver conditions** generate increased thirst, as do many internal infections and endocrine-system diseases (see Chapter 6, Hair and Skin). A decrease in thirst is a less common sign of illness and usually is connected to pain or nausea: Your pet isn't drinking because it hurts to swallow (see Chapter 5, Mouth and Throat) or to urinate, or because she has learned that drinking is accompanied by nausea and vomiting.

On the topic of urination, a change in the amount of liquid your pet drinks is quite often accompanied by a change in her elimination habits. To know whether your dog is urinating abnormally, however, you first must know what is "normal" for your particular animal. Admittedly this can be tough if yours is an outside pooch; easier if your dog "does her business" when you take her for daily walks. Either way, it's important to keep abreast of your dog's elimination activity, since a problem with it is a reliable indicator of a condition involving the kidneys, urinary tract, hormones, or other internal organs.

The word "irregular" can refer to a change in the color of the urine or frequency of elimination habits, obvious pain while voiding, or the presence of blood, mucous, or grit in the urine. Often one of these irregularities will be the only sign that your dog's health is off. Other times, your pooch may also exhibit easier-to-see signs, such as abdomen distension or vomiting.

Cloudy, Bloody Urine, Accompanied by a Pained Expression When Urinating

RELATED SYMPTOMS: Attempts to urinate may be more urgent, yet only a few drops will be yielded. Occasionally, you may see clotted blood and/or gravelly stones in the urine, or you may see heavy bleeding with each attempt to void.

POSSIBLE CAUSE: Is your pet a female? Or an older male? Both are prone to **urinary-tract infections**—females because infection-carrying bacteria can travel more easily up the shorter urethra into the bladder, and older males because they often suffer from enlarged prostates, which press on and irritate the bladder, making complete emptying of the bladder more difficult.

In some cases, bladder infections can prompt the formation of small stones—especially in susceptible breeds like boxers, poodles, dalmatians, dachshunds, German shepherds, pugs, and Irish and cairn terriers. These grow in the bladder and can become as large as golf balls, irritating the bladder wall and causing constant bleeding.

CARE: If your pet is bleeding with each attempt to urinate, take her to the vet. Otherwise, if bleeding is very sporadic, you can attempt to treat the condition yourself for a short time. The secret is to encourage your pet to drink large amounts of liquid. Increased fluid intake helps flush the area of guilty bacteria and dilutes the urine for less-painful voiding (concentrated urine often burns as it travels through the urethra). As unorthodox as it sounds, you can nudge your pooch to drink more by salting her food, thus making her thirsty. (However, if a kidney or heart problem is suspected or present, adding salt is not advised.) Cranberry juice (either mixed in with your dog's food or directly administered to the mouth) stops certain bacteria from adhering to the bladder wall, consequently reducing the level of bacteria present. Ascorbic acid is also helpful for acidifying urine, as well as building up the immune system, and vitamin A is useful in strengthening the mucosal lining of the bladder (see Appendix E, List of Recommended Dosages, pp. 200–223).

If the dog bleeds with each attempt to void or shows no improvement in 24 hours, take her to the vet, who will analyze the urine. If a urethral, bladder, or kidney infection is the culprit, your pet will be placed on antibiotics. Small stones can be nudged through the urethra by a loop catheter; larger stones require surgical removal.

PREVENTION: To help prevent bladder infections, make sure the dog is given an opportunity to urinate at least every 6 to 8 hours. The longer urine is retained in the bladder, the more likely it is to become alkaline and to develop an infection. Provide plenty of drinking water to keep the bladder flushed of bacteria and to encourage frequent urination. If yours is a longhaired pooch, keep the genital-area fur clipped to make it harder for bacteria to congregate there.

Difficult Bowel Movements, Fever, and a Frequent Urge to Defecate, Possibly Accompanied by Blood and/or Pus in the Urine

RELATED SYMPTOMS: The dog may also have a painful abdomen, accompanied by lameness in the hind limbs.

POSSIBLE CAUSE: Is your pet a male who is older than seven? Is he unneutered? If one or both of these describe your pooch, he could have a **prostate disorder**. It's not uncommon for older males—especially those who haven't been fixed—to develop an **enlarged prostate gland** or to suffer from a **bacterial infection, cyst,** or **tumor of the prostate gland**. All these conditions can cause the gland to become inflamed and press against the nearby rectum, making defecation uncomfortable.

To make things worse—literally—a stricken dog typically strains to eliminate, which can cause a hernia. Furthermore, an enlarged prostate can also lead to kidney and bladder inflammation, abscesses, and cysts.

CARE: Although not an acute emergency, a prostate disorder does need veterinary attention. Therefore, make an appointment with your vet for the upcoming week. In the meantime, your goal should be to make defecating more comfortable for your pet. Enter: the special "easy-digest" diet—3 parts cooked rice to 1 part low-fat or fat-free cottage cheese mixed with 1 teaspoon vegetable oil.

Your vet will perform a rectal examination and/or a radiograph in order to determine the size and tenderness of the prostate and reach a diagnosis. Estrogen treatments can shrink an enlarged prostate until the dog is neutered, after which the gland should shrink by itself. If a tumor, cyst, or abscess is present, surgery will often be necessary to solve the problem. In the case of infection, the vet will recommend antibiotics to prevent the condition from spreading to the kidneys.

PREVENTION: Neuter your dog.

Increased Thirst and Urination, Vomiting, Weight Loss, Lethargy, and Dehydration

RELATED SYMPTOMS: The animal is apathetic, her breath smells like urine, and she seems either dazed or in a state of heightened excitability. The vomit may contain blood, and the stool is often dark and soft. The urine is very light in color and very dilute.

POSSIBLE CAUSE: Is yours an older animal? Has she ingested poison at some time in the past? At some point in her life has she been on a long course (a month or more) of antibiotics? Has she ever been diagnosed with heat stroke, heart disease, repeat urinary-tract infections, periodontal disease, or an autoimmune disease? A "yes" to any one of these can indicate **chronic kidney disease** (as opposed to acute kidney disease, which is discussed in the next section).

Unlike acute kidney failure, kidney disease is a slowly developing impairment that hinders the kidneys' ability to concentrate urine and filter toxins from the blood. As kidney cells die—whether naturally or through chemicals or undue strain—they are replaced by scar tissue, which is useless at cleaning blood. In the disease's later stages, chronic kidney failure can occur.

CARE: Take your dog to the vet, who will conduct blood and/or urine tests to diagnose the condition. The disease must be distinguished from a number of other diseases that cause excess drinking and urination, particularly diabetes. Severe cases will be treated with intravenous fluids and a special low-protein diet. Antibiotics will be used if infection is present.

A dog with kidney disease should be kept as stress-free as possible in order to keep the body, and thus the kidneys, from having to work harder than necessary. A constant supply of fresh water should be available to the pooch, since even slight dehydration could prompt the kidneys to fail or make already existing kidney failure more severe. Increased drinking also helps flush the kidneys and remove toxin buildup. Because your dog will be urinating more, antioxidant vitamins A and C (in the form of calcium ascorbate, not ascorbic acid) may be prescribed to supplant those nutrients lost in the increased urine flow. Other antioxidants and anabolic steroids may be prescribed. Be sure to feed your dog a high-quality, chemical-free, low-protein diet that is not acidic.

PREVENTION: Address any urinary-tract illness immediately and supply adequate water. Pay attention to your pet's drinking and elimination habits in order to detect changes early. Reduction of toxins in the pet's environment and in her food may slow progressive kidney damage.

Increased Thirst, Greatly Reduced Urine Output, Dark and/or Bloody Urine, and a Swollen Abdomen

RELATED SYMPTOMS: The dog may not be urinating at all. The abdomen and loin area hurt and the animal may be feverish, apathetic, and may refuse to eat. She may retch, even when she has no food in her stomach. Her breath may be sour and smell like urine.

POSSIBLE CAUSE: Has your dog recently been in an accident where she lost a lot of blood? Could she have ingested rat poison, antifreeze, or any other kidney-damaging substance during an unsupervised moment? Has she suffered from stones in, or an injury to, the urinary-tract system? Has she recently wrestled with a bout of heavy diarrhea and vomiting? Has she been on antibiotics recently? Has she been diagnosed with a serious abdominal infection, such as peritonitis or pyometra? A nod to any of these may indicate **acute kidney failure.** The condition occurs when kidney cells are badly injured or killed off due to chemicals, bacteria, or extreme strain caused from overuse, which results in the organ's inability to filter toxins from the blood.

CARE: Take your dog to a vet immediately. A blood and/or urine test can detect kidney failure. If her kidneys are failing, your pet will be given intravenous fluids and medications to stimulate kidney function. Your vet will then determine the underlying cause of the kidney failure and treat it.

PREVENTION: Supervise your dog's elimination behavior and address all symptoms promptly. Don't let your dog get into your—or your neighbors'—garbage.

Repeated, Uncontrolled Passing of Urine in an Otherwise Housebroken Dog

RELATED SYMPTOM: Dog repeatedly urinates in inappropriate spots, such as in the house.

POSSIBLE CAUSE: Has your dog been spayed in the past few months? Is your pet an older animal? Has she been diagnosed with a herniated disc, urinary-tract condition, or weakness of the bladder sphincter muscles? Answering "yes" to any of these may indicate **incontinence.**

Incontinence can be blamed on anything from age to illness. Spaying your dog can, in rare instances, create a hormone deficiency that results in urinary incontinence. To further complicate matters, often the culprit is not physical at all, but psychological. Perhaps the dog is nervous or angry about an upset in her routine or living conditions, or maybe she's suffering from separation anxiety. Because animals can't verbally complain about what's upsetting them, they may show their unhappiness by soiling their owners' living quarters and possessions. If you suspect that a change in routine or separation anxiety is to blame for your dog's free-flowing urine, see section in Chapter 2, Inappropriate Elimination Habits, pp. 19–20.

CARE: Before going to a vet, consider your dog's age. As we—and this includes all mammals—approach our golden years, our ability to hold urine for long periods of time decreases. Simply put, we need to void more often. If yours is an older pooch, try adding an extra walk to her day or let her outside for an additional play session. You may also want to supplement your pet's diet with high-quality lecithin (see Appendix E, List of Recommended Dosages, pp. 200–223), which may help to strengthen the bladder and consequently reduce the likelihood of leaking urine.

If this doesn't correct the situation or you can't find a reason for your pet's behavior, visit your vet, who will search for an underlying medical cause. If there is a physical cause for the incontinence, treatment will depend on what is causing it. Hormones and other medications are available to strengthen weakened sphincters.

PREVENTION: You can't prevent an incontinence-causing illness, however, you can help an older pet by allowing her frequent access to the outdoors.

Disorders of Sex Organs

Unfixed dogs of both sexes are more likely to suffer from infectious diseases and other physical conditions involving reproductive organs. Why? Because these unneutered animals have more organs to be affected. The reproductive parts of both sexes can be strained, injured, or infected by a number of conditions related to sexual activity, in addition to females going through heat, pregnancy, and lactation.

Only a portion of your dog's reproductive system is external. Called genitalia, these sexual parts are easily monitored for physical changes. Perhaps a testicle will look swollen, or the vulva will be inflamed. (Although breasts are not categorized as genitalia, their size and firmness are directly affected by certain sex hormones such that a breast that is hard to the touch can be a useful symptom to consider when diagnosing a disease in a sex organ.)

Then there are instances when the foreskin (prepuce), vulva, and/or breasts will look normal, or perhaps only slightly swollen, but will excrete some type of discharge. This material can be milky, clear, greenish, or yellowish. It may or may not contain mucous, blood, or pus, and there may be a lot of it or very little. Other than the dog constantly licking the stuff away, this discharge might be the sole sign that something is amiss with the interior reproductive organs (although discharge can be accompanied by pain, changes in urination, abdominal enlargement, or lethargy).

In females, a vaginal discharge often signals pregnancy-related problems, such as **placental disease,** the **uterus's failure to repair itself after delivery,** or a **uterine infection** (such as **pyometritis**). In males, **trauma to the genitals, infections of the penis and foreskin,** and **prostate disorders** are the leading cause of discharge. To determine exactly what is causing the discharge, however, your vet will physically examine your pet and study the discharge's content microscopically.

Blood-Tinged Discharge from the Vulva More Than Six Weeks After Giving Birth

RELATED SYMPTOMS: Thin, blood-tinged discharge is normal during the first 6 weeks after giving birth. The passing of bright blood or any excretions occurring more than a 1½ months after delivering is not. The passage of pus during the first 6 weeks is *not* normal and the dog should be seen by a vet immediately.

POSSIBLE CAUSE: Has your dog given birth in the last

6 weeks? It's possible that she has a condition called **uterine subinvolution.** In layperson's language, this means the uterus is not properly repairing itself after the birthing process. The condition can lead to anemia and uterine infections.

CARE: Take your dog to the vet, who will make a diagnosis after studying your dog's physical condition and examining the discharge microscopically. If the bleeding is mild, the uterus may simply be taking its time repairing itself and will finish healing after 2 or 2½ months; in extreme cases, the uterus may have to be removed. Regardless of the bleeding's severity, iron supplements are typically prescribed to ward off anemia. If an infection is present, antibiotics will also be prescribed.

PREVENTION: Spay your dog in order to prevent further pregnancies.

Excessive Licking of the Female Genitals, Vaginal Discharge, and Dragging the Rear End Along the Ground

RELATED SYMPTOMS: The discharge may contain blood, pus, or mucous. The outer folds of the vagina will appear large and swollen, and the inner vagina may protrude. You may also notice appetite loss, lethargy, vomiting, increased water intake, fever, abdominal pain, and weakness in your dog's hind legs.

POSSIBLE CAUSE: Is your pet sexually active? Has she recently given birth? Has she been diagnosed with a metabolic disease like diabetes, or is she being treated with progesterone-based medication? Any of these can point to an **infection of the reproductive tract,** usually the vagina or uterus. Of course, keep in mind her normal reproductive cycle and consider the possibility she simply may be in heat.

CARE: Take your pet to the vet, who will take a bacterial culture and/or X rays to reach a diagnosis. Antibiotics will be prescribed, which can either be applied topically via a douche infusion, administered orally, or injected. If dehydration is present—this is more common with an infected uterus—intravenous fluids will also be given. If there are any nursing puppies, they will be transferred to a formula diet.

A severely infected uterus (also known as pyometritis) in an unspayed female will prompt your vet to recommend spaying. Spaying is essentially an ovariohysterectomy and involves removing the ovaries and most of the uterus. The rationale? Spaying your pet will prevent the condition from recurring—an important step, since uterus infections often recur and can lead to liver and kidney damage, or even to a ruptured uterus.

PREVENTION: Since many reproductive-tract infections are caused by sexual activity, consider having your dog fixed or strictly confining her during her heat periods.

One or More Lumps or Flat Patches on a Breast

RELATED SYMPTOMS: These might be ulcerated. If one lump is noticed, check all other mammary glands on both sides for more lumps.

POSSIBLE CAUSE: Is your dog a female older than seven? Has she had two or more pregnancies (or false pregnancies), or has she ever received hormones to prevent estrus? Is she unspayed? If you can answer "yes" to any of these, your pooch may have **breast tumors.** This isn't uncommon: Half of all tumors in older females occur in the mammary glands, usually on the rear breasts.

CARE: Immediate vet care is the most prudent path. Some owners may want to wait a week and see if the lump "goes down" before going to the vet. However, I do not recommend waiting a week since the sooner a diagnosis is made, the better the prognosis.

Your vet may surgically take a tissue sample or remove the entire lump to learn whether the lump is malignant. If it is, an X ray will determine whether the cancer has spread to the lungs. If it has, it is too late to operate; your vet will discuss how long your dog may live and ways to make her remaining time comfortable. If the cancer is limited to the breasts or the lumps are benign, the growths and the surrounding tissue will be removed. After surgery, be sure that your dog does not scratch, paw, or bite her incision: An Elizabethan collar may help to restrain your dog from touching the incision until after it has healed and the sutures are removed.

PREVENTION: Spay your dog. Research has shown that dogs spayed before 18 months have the lowest incidence of breast tumors.

Painful, Swollen, Warm Breasts in a Dog with Puppies

RELATED SYMPTOMS: The condition may exist in one, some, or all breasts. A watery, puslike, or even bloody secretion leaks from the nipples when pressure is placed on the breasts. The breast feels firm or even hard. The dog frequently has a fever.

POSSIBLE CAUSE: Is your dog nursing? Are her puppies rough when nursing? Does she have trouble releasing milk from all nipples? She may have **mastitis**, a bacterial infection of the mammary glands. The condition develops when glands are damaged by coagulated milk, poor hygiene, a uterine infection, or injuries inflicted by hungry puppies.

CARE: If there is no bloody discharge and the area is only slightly swollen, massage the affected breasts 2 times a day with rubbing alcohol or a mentholated camphor ointment to increase circulation and lower the skin temperature. You can also apply hot packs (*not scalding*) and express the gland to draw out some of the coagulated and caked milk. Do not let the pups nurse on the affected glands (you can prevent them from doing so by placing adhesive tape over the infected nipples or by applying a belly band). Aspirin can be given to relieve the dog's pain (give a 10-pound dog 81mg of baby aspirin).

If blood is being secreted, or if the condition of breasts doesn't improve after 48 hours with this homecare, take your pet to the vet, who will give your dog a diagnostic exam. If the breasts are abscessed, your pooch will be put under anesthesia so the vet can lance, drain, clean, and bandage the glands. Antibiotics will also be given and the puppies will be taken off the mother and placed on a formula diet.

PREVENTION: Check your nursing dog's breasts daily. Because an infection can be passed on to puppies, any change in breast conditions should be addressed immediately and the infants placed on formula or prevented from using their mother's affected gland(s).

Redness and Inflammation of One or Both Testicles, and a Stiff Gait with Straddled Hind Legs

RELATED SYMPTOMS: The scrotal area will be painful to the touch, and the scrotum may even be abscessed and filled with foul-smelling pus. The dog may have a fever and/or refuse to eat.

POSSIBLE CAUSE: Does your dog spend unsupervised time outside? Has he recently suffered a groin injury or scrape to the testicles? A "yes" to either of these questions could indicate **orchitis**, also known by the less medical-sounding **inflammation of the testicles**.

CARE: If the area is simply swollen and red without the presence of abscesses, you can attempt home treatment. Prepare a large batch of chamomile tea; let it cool to room temperature. Gently swabbing the area 3 times daily with this liquid can help keep the inflammation in check, as can following the tea applications with zinc ointment, available at drugstores or from your vet.

If an abscess appears to be present—or if you see no improvement in 48 hours of homecare—take your dog to the vet, who will prescribe antibiotics. If your pooch can't stop licking himself, your vet will fit him with an Elizabethan collar. This plastic, funnel-like contraption is worn around the neck and makes it virtually impossible for your pet to reach his backside. If the condition is severe enough, surgical lancing and drainage, or even castration, may be indicated.

PREVENTION: Supervise your dog's time outdoors. To ward off infection, treat any injuries, even small cuts and scrapes, immediately. If you are not interested in breeding your dog, consider castration.

Testicles Absent in the Scrotum Sac in an Unfixed Male

RELATED SYMPTOMS: The scrotum will either be empty (a condition known medically as **cryptorchidism**) or it may appear as if your dog has what vets call **monorchidism** (which means one testicle).

POSSIBLE CAUSE: Was your dog this way from birth? Is he a young dog? He probably has a retained testicle or testicles, a condition present at birth. Instead of being suspended in the scrotum, the **testicle(s) are stuck in the abdominal cavity**.

CARE: Take your pooch to the vet, who will go into the abdominal cavity and surgically remove the testicle(s). These "interior" testicles have a higher incidence of cancer and are more prone to infections than normal "externally worn" testicles.

PREVENTION: There is no prevention.

Pregnancy

A female dog is usually sexually mature between six and nine months of age. If she is not fixed, she will go through estrus (commonly known as "heat") 2 times a year. Estrus lasts 2 to 3 weeks: If your dog is going to get pregnant, this is the time she'll do it.

A vet can usually tell your dog is pregnant 4 weeks after conception or breeding by simply feeling her belly. Not only will it be heavier, but you may feel the ripples of unborn puppies. Because a canine pregnancy only lasts 60 to 65 days, the whole process is much more accelerated than a human pregnancy. Thus, it's important to visit a vet as soon as you suspect your dog is expecting. Your vet will examine your pooch and may place her on a special diet along with other nutritional supplements.

At 45 days, an X ray can tell how many puppies your dog is carrying. She will become more and more sedentary, while eating more and more. In fact, in the last 2 weeks of her pregnancy, your pooch may be eating up to three times what she ate before becoming pregnant. During this later stage, your dog will also want to prepare a nesting area where she'll give birth and later attend to her puppies. Your vet can help you by offering guidelines and suggesting suit able nesting material (such as blankets and towels) for your particular dog's needs.

Signs that your pet will be giving birth within the next 24 hours include a drop in body temperature to as low as 98°F and little interest in food. She may spend almost all her time sitting in the nest you've provided for her waiting for labor to begin, leaving only to relieve herself. During this time she may shred the bedding you've provided for her, claw at the floor of the nesting area, and even tear out her own fur. This is completely normal: She's trying to make the area softer and more comfortable for both herself (after all, she's got a long day in front of her) and her soon-to-be-born offspring.

The birthing process is a wondrous experience, so it's tempting to ask people to share it with you and your pet. However, remember that this is a physically and mentally challenging time for your pooch. She's in pain, she's working hard, and she doesn't need the added emotional strain of having strangers—or, for that matter, too many human family members—watching the action. Someone should certainly watch her progress, but limit the number of humans in the room to two.

As labor approaches, your dog may tremble and pant. Her pulse rate will increase and milk may leak from her nipples. If it has been more than twenty-four hours since she first started exhibiting these signs and you don't notice visible contractions that signal the birthing process, **call your vet immediately**.

Contractions are strong, visible, straining movements, which involve both the abdominal muscles and diaphragm. A small amount of tan fluid excreted by the vulva may accompany the contractions. This is active labor and during it your dog may either lie on her side or her sternum (chest), or she may squat (a position resembling defecation). If, after 1 hour of this straining, no puppy appears, **call your vet**. A puppy could be stuck in the birth canal or the head may be too large for natural birth. Be aware that because smaller dogs (such as Pekingese, Chihuahuas, or Yorkshire terriers) often have very difficult labors, your vet may recommend a cesarean delivery.

In a normal birth, babies emerge 30 to 60 minutes apart, each newborn followed by the afterbirth (placenta). Your dog will eat the membrane that encases the newly born pup, then chew off the umbilical cords. She'll then give each pup a good lickdown. Not only does this clean the puppies, it also stimulates their circulation and encourages them to nurse.

If, for some reason, your dog does not eat the encasing membrane, you will have to break open the sac so the puppy can breathe. Use your *clean* fingers and gently tear the membrane away. Should the mother fail to sever the umbilical cord, you can wait until after she's done delivering to see if she will get around to it. If she doesn't, get a clean piece of sewing thread or unwaxed dental floss and tie it around the cord 1 inch from the puppy's body. Then, cut (using a *disinfected* pair of scissors) or break (using your fingers) the cord just past the thread or floss.

After giving birth your dog will rest and nurse her pups. Her appetite may take a few long hours to return, but she may want water.

It should be noted that veterinary professionals routinely urge pet owners to get their female *and* male dogs neutered. Not only are neutered pets less prone to ailments involving the reproductive organs, they are less likely to exhibit sexually based behavior problems like roaming or aggression. Another very good argument for having your female or male dog neutered is the staggering number of unwanted dogs in America: Each day, hundreds of thousands of dogs are either abandoned by owners who no longer want them or put to sleep by overcrowded pounds. In order not to contribute to this avoidable tragedy, it is important to keep your pet from breeding unless you are certain of good, solid, loving, compatible homes for all your dog's off-spring.

Dark Red or Black Fluid Excreted from the Vaginal Canal with No Following Birth and/or More Than an Hour Between the Emergence of Each Puppy

RELATED SYMPTOMS: Your dog may show an excessive amount of discomfort. Although this can be hard to gauge, considering giving birth is an extremely uncomfortable situation, be sensitive to crying, yelping, or vomiting.

POSSIBLE CAUSE: Your dog may be suffering from **dystocia**: In other words, she's having a difficult labor. This can be caused by puppies whose heads are too big for your dog's birth canal, a large puppy or afterbirth stuck in the birth canal, or a puppy positioned awkwardly.

CARE: Call your vet at the first sign of trouble. He may make a house call or he may talk you through the process over the phone. Typically, here's what you might be told: Wash your hands with antibacterial soap or dish soap, then lubricate a finger with petroleum jelly and insert that finger into the vaginal canal. You should feel a puppy. Can you figure out where the head and front and rear legs are? Often a puppy's leg will bend under itself, causing it to become stuck. If that feels like it may be the case, you can reposition the leg. Remember, for your pooch's comfort, *be gentle!*

If the puppy seems to be in a normal position, you can help ease her through the canal by gently grasping the puppy around the shoulders. You don't want to put pressure on her head, neither should you tug on the amniotic sac surrounding her. Wait for the mother's natural contractions.

When one strikes, softly pull the puppy downward (this is the direction the vagina is angled). If the pup's head seems too large to fit through your pet's vulva, there's a chance you can very gently finesse the edges of the vulva to fit around the puppy's head (if not, your vet will need to perform an emergency episiotomy, an incision into the tissues surrounding the opening of the vagina in order to enlarge it).

In some cases, retained placenta is blocking the delivery of the next pup. Using the same steps just outlined, you can often find this afterbirth. Grasp it, and gently but firmly pull until it passes out of the vaginal canal. After this, your pet may not be ready to deliver the next pup right away. She may need a prolonged rest period before the next puppy is delivered.

PREVENTION: Dogs who have one difficult birth tend to repeat the experience the next time they get pregnant. To prevent this painful scenario, consider having your dog spayed.

Sexual Behavior Abnormalities

Not all sexual conditions have physical symptoms. You may notice your dog acting differently, thus signaling something is wrong with part of the reproductive system you can't see. A well-known example is the oversexed male who—much to his owner's dismay—mounts everything from furniture to visiting neighbors to other animals. No, this isn't everyday male dog behavior. It's caused by too many male sex hormones, and it can be treated, as can other abnormal sexual behaviors, including roaming (males) and mothering toys (females). Aggression may or may not be categorized as sexual.

As with symptoms involving the genitals, sexual-based behavioral symptoms are much less common in dogs who have been neutered. It used to be thought that the youngest age a dog should be neutered is 6 months. However, many humane societies and veterinarians are now neutering as young as 8 to 12 weeks—an important fact, because the younger the dog is when neutered, the less run-ins you'll have later with these behaviors and conditions. In addition, research has shown that fixing animals before they reach one year affords protection from reproductive-tract cancers, uterine diseases in females, and prostate conditions in males.

Aggression, with Frequent Attempts to Mount People, Other Dogs, and Inanimate Objects

RELATED SYMPTOMS: Your dog may wander excessively and constantly mark territory.

POSSIBLE CAUSE: Is your dog an unneutered male? There's a good chance he is suffering from **hypersexuality** caused by an overproduction of male hormones.

CARE: Neutering is the ultimate solution. If, for some reason, that isn't an acceptable option, your vet can try to temporarily keep your dog's aggression in check by prescribing estrogen. This is especially important when there are unneutered females in the neighborhood.

PREVENTION: Neuter your dog, or at least keep him confined so that he does not jump the fence to breed with neighborhood females in heat. An aggressive dog is a serious danger to children, adults, and to other roaming dogs, so be a responsible owner and make sure the problem is quickly addressed. A good dog-training class will teach you how to dominate your dog and remain in charge.

Defending of Toys by a Nonpregnant, Unmated Female, Nest-Building, and Enlarged Breasts

RELATED SYMPTOMS: If pressure is applied to the breasts, the nipples secrete milk. You may also notice aggressive behavior, a tendency to hide in quiet places, and a change in appetite. All symptoms take place 6 to 8 weeks *after* your dog has experienced estrus (being in heat).

POSSIBLE CAUSE: Has your dog recently gone through heat? Are you positive that she has not mated during an unsupervised moment? She may be experiencing **false pregnancy** (known in vetspeak as **pseudocyesis**). After estrus, a dog's progesterone levels remain high for up to 10 weeks, even if she has not mated. These higher hormone levels lead some females to wrongly feel that they are pregnant, and their body functions and behavior imitate that condition.

CARE: There is no way through physical observation that you can tell false pregnancy apart from the early stages of real pregnancy. Unless you are absolutely, positively, 100 percent sure that your dog has not slipped out and mated while in heat or that a male dog didn't jump the fence, there's always the chance that she is pregnant. If you know she's not, your goal is to make her "snap out of it." This should take no longer than 3 weeks.

Massage her breasts with diluted rubbing alcohol to stimulate circulation to the area and reduce swelling. Keep her distracted by extending her walking schedule and playtime. Remove all "nesting materials," such as blankets, pillows, and towels. If she's adopted any toys or shoes as surrogate puppies, take those away, too.

Should her breasts become inflamed, or if she's still behaving this way after 3 weeks (or you're truly unsure whether she's expecting), take her to your vet. He can give her a hormone injection to help shorten the duration of this condition. A diagnostic ultrasound or X rays can reveal the presence—or nonpresence—of puppies. X rays are incapable of detecting the fetus before the 45th day of pregnancy.

PREVENTION: Dogs who are troubled by false pregnancy are more likely to develop other reproductive disorders, such as uterine infections. Unless you are determined to get a litter of pups from your dog, you would be wise to have her neutered.

Nervousness, Pacing, Whining, and Trembling in a Pregnant Dog or Nursing Mother

RELATED SYMPTOMS: The animal will have a fever and respiratory problems and might appear uncoordinated, have muscle spasms, and pant. The condition could be mistaken for an epileptic seizure.

POSSIBLE CAUSE: Is your dog due to have puppies in the next 2 weeks? Or has she given birth within the last 3 weeks? She may be suffering from **eclampsia,** a serious condition caused by reduced blood-calcium levels. The illness typically strikes small dogs.

CARE: **Take your pet immediately to the vet.** The accompanying high fevers and respiratory troubles can lead to death. Your vet can reach a diagnosis by observing the just-mentioned clinical signs and analyzing the blood for low blood-calcium levels. Fortunately, eclampsia is easily treated with intravenous calcium and cortisone injections. If your dog has puppies, they will be placed on formula, so that they no longer steal the mother's calcium.

In the event that you are unable to get to the vet right away, give your pet Gatorade or an infant electrolyte solution such as Pedialyte (see Appendix E, List of Recommended Dosages, pp. 200–223). Due to continual seizures that result from low blood-calcium levels, the dog's temperature may elevate to dangerous levels (over 104.5°F); if this occurs before you get to a vet, follow the care recommended in Chapter 1 for fever and heat stroke (see pp. 11–12).

PREVENTION: If your pet is pregnant, especially if she is a small dog, talk to your vet about calcium supplements. Feed a pregnant or nursing dog a diet high in calcium to prevent the onset of eclampsia: Yogurt, cottage cheese, and dark green vegetables are all good sources of calcium. Providing the nursing mother with a vitamin-mineral supplement (recommended by your vet) which contains the proper ratio of calcium to phosphorus is also a good idea. Exposure to natural sunlight will help the dog's body to better absorb calcium from the intestinal tract.

Vomiting

In humans, vomiting is a scary symptom. Not only is it supremely uncomfortable, it usually accompanies some kind of problem, such as a flu, anorexia, a high blood-alcohol level, motion sickness, food poisoning, or an overdose of medication. In dogs, however, vomiting isn't always a cause for alarm. Pooches often throw up after snacking on grass, accidentally ingesting an irritant, or wolfing down more dinner—in a shorter period of time—than their stomachs are ready for.

So how do you distinguish "neutral vomiting" from vomiting that signals a medical condition? Severity. Vomiting 1 or 2 times total is *not* considered severe. Vomiting continually for 1 hour straight, or on and off for 24 hours or more, is severe. Vomiting that persists or recurs over the course of several days or that increases in frequency over a week should receive prompt veterinary attention. Besides indicating a medical problem, the vomiting itself can cause an additional problem of its own: severe dehydration.

The presence of other symptoms helps your vet diagnose your pet's condition. When containing blood or mucous, vomiting is usually a result of gastrointestinal disease or possibly the presence of an intestinal foreign body. When joined by severe abdominal pain, it can point to infection or disease of other abdominal organs. When accompanied by dark urine and a refusal to eat, kidney disease can be the culprit. When seen with diarrhea and respiratory signs, distemper may be to blame (see section in Chapter 7, Constant Cough, Possibly Accompanied by Fever, Lethargy, and a Combination of Eye/Nasal Discharge, Diarrhea, Vomiting, and Muscle Spasms, pp. 94–96).

This is a good time to mention what vomiting is *not*: regurgitation. Vomiting is the forceful ejection of food and/ or fluid. Regurgitation is passive; food "just comes up"—

not from the stomach or duodenum as with vomiting, but from the esophagus.

Chronic Vomiting, Lack of Appetite, and Lethargy

RELATED SYMPTOMS: You might notice bits of curdled blood in the dog's vomit, and the animal may have a painful abdomen and thus shrink from being touched there. The feces may be dark or even black, indicating the presence of blood.

POSSIBLE CAUSES: Has your dog been under stress? Has she swallowed a sharp object or ingested a caustic substance? Does she have a metabolic or infectious disease? Has she been diagnosed with internal parasites? A "yes" to any of these seemingly unrelated questions can signal an **ulcer** or a **stomach tumor.**

Rather than being a primary condition, ulcers are actually a sign of another underlying condition. They are produced by an overabundance of gastric acid that erodes the gastrointestinal lining. What causes tumors, however, isn't known, although it's suspected that chronic stomach inflammation contributes to their growth.

CARE: Your vet will perform a radiograph or endoscopic exam to determine if ulcers or tumors are present. For ulcers, the underlying cause will be treated. The dog will also receive medication to reduce the stomach acid, thus giving the ulcerated areas a chance to heal. Many stomach ulcers are caused by a bacteria known as *Helicobacter*, which can be effectively eliminated by antibiotics. If tumors are present, your vet may operate to remove them.

PREVENTION: If administered on a permanent basis, drugs that check the production of gastric acid can prevent ulcers. Small meals of low-fat food given 3 or 4 times a day also may be helpful.

Constant Vomiting, Trembling, and Foul-Smelling Diarrhea That Is Foamy and Mixed with Bright Red Blood

RELATED SYMPTOMS: The dog's temperature will alternate between being very high and below-normal. She will appear apathetic, have little appetite, and suffer from abdominal pain. You may hear rumbling from her intestines.

POSSIBLE CAUSE: Does your dog spend time outdoors in the company of neighborhood pooches? Is your pet a puppy who you found as a stray or adopted from a pound? It's possible that she has been infected with canine **parvovirus,** an infectious virus that damages the mucous lining of the small intestine. Most frequently seen in puppies under six months old, it does hit dogs of all ages. The condition usually lasts from 4 days to 2 weeks and—if your pooch is suffering a particularly severe bout—can cause death.

CARE: A dog who survives the first week of being infected with canine parvovirus is usually out of danger. This means that if you suspect the condition, you should go immediately to your vet because parvovirus can be mistaken for distemper (see section in Chapter 7, Constant Cough, Possibly Accompanied by Fever, Lethargy, and a Combination of Eye/Nasal Discharge, Diarrhea, Vomiting, and Muscle Spasms, pp. 94–96). In addition to a thorough physical, he will also need to perform tests on the dog's blood and stool in order to diagnose the condition. To keep the already-strained small intestines from being further taxed, the dog must be fasted for at least 2 days, during which time your dog will need to be hospitalized. During the fast, the vet gives intravenous fluid replacement to prevent dehydration and administers medication to control the dog's vomiting and diarrhea. He will also place your pup on antibiotics. At home, you must thoroughly clean and disinfect all surfaces and bedding. Also, you must slowly reintroduce food—your vet will discuss this with you.

PREVENTION: Limit your dog's contact with unknown dogs. Make sure your dog is routinely vaccinated against parvovirus.

Vomiting, Dazed Demeanor, and Increased Thirst

RELATED SYMPTOMS: The vomit may be bloody and might occur more frequently soon after drinking. Your dog may feel pain in her abdomen, and you may hear a distinct rumbling from her stomach.

POSSIBLE CAUSE: Does your pet have a food allergy or sensitivity? Has she eaten spoiled food or ingested a poisonous or irritating substance or foreign body? A "yes" to either of these questions might signal **gastritis,** an inflammation of the stomach.

CARE: If the vomiting isn't constant, try withholding food for a full 24 hours. Provide small amounts of Gatorade or sugar water (1 part maple syrup or uncarbonated soda to 3 parts water) frequently (approximately every 15 minutes), but prevent consumption of large amounts of fluid all at once, which may stimulate vomiting. Chamomile tea (1 teaspoon to 1 tablespoon 2 times a day) is also recommended. If your dog keeps this down, try placing the dog on a low-protein, limited-fat, high-carbohydrate diet. Try combining 7 parts rice to 3 parts diced chicken and adding 1 teaspoon vegetable oil, or you may feed the dog a combination of cooked hamburger/white rice or cottage cheese/white rice. Divvy this into 4 small daily meals.

But if there is no improvement after 24 hours, take your dog to the vet, who will perform a physical exam and laboratory tests, and take X rays. If vomiting is frequent or constant, then take your dog to the vet immediately.

Intravenous feeding of a saline-electrolyte solution will prevent dehydration. An antacid may be given to neutralize or stop the production of gastric acid.

PREVENTION: Keep a close watch on your dog's diet. Consider serving 3 or 4 smaller meals instead of 1 or 2 larger ones. A hypoallergenic diet may be in order.

Vomiting, Diarrhea, Excess Salivation, and Pain on the Right Side of the Abdomen Directly Behind the Rib Cage

RELATED SYMPTOMS: The dog shows no interest in food and appears depressed. To alleviate pain, your pet may strike a prayer pose: bended front legs and an elevated rump.

POSSIBLE CAUSE: Is your pooch middle-aged and overweight? Does she eat a high-fat diet and/or an abundance of table scraps? Is she a schnauzer? Is your dog female? A "yes" to any one of these questions might indicate **pancreatitis,** an extremely painful ailment marked by overproduction of pancreatic digestive enzymes, which begins to damage the pancreatic tissue itself.

CARE: In extreme cases, pancreatitis can be so excruciating that pain-induced shock and death result. In other words, take your dog to the vet. To determine whether she has pancreatitis and not gastric dilation-volvulus complex (GDV) or an intestinal obstruction—both of which feature similar signs—your vet will perform a radiograph and blood tests to measure the level of pancreatic enzymes.

If pancreatitis is the problem, your vet will order all food and water to be discontinued for up to 72 hours. This fast will lower the number of digestive enzymes the pancreas manufactures. To prevent dehydration, your dog will be given intravenous fluids, while special medication will reduce pancreatic secretions that can cause secondary complications.

Unfortunately, once a dog comes down with pancreatitis, there's a good chance of periodic recurrence. As a preventative measure, your vet will place your dog on an easily digestible, extremely low-fat daily diet, which doesn't tax the pancreas.

PREVENTION: Feed your dog a low-fat, high-fiber, chemical-free diet with lots of raw vegetables (such as corn and grated cabbage), but avoid giving her fruit (because we want the dog to have complex carbohydrates, not simple sugars). Supplement the diet with antioxidants such as vitamins E and C (calcium ascorbate) (see Appendix E, List of Recommended Dosages, pp. 200–223). Never give her "people food," and don't let her become overweight. Never give your pet fat-laden chicken or turkey skin, and keep the garbage can securely covered or out of sight. Encourage your dog to get plenty of exercise.

Vomiting, Diarrhea with a Light-Colored Stool, Tiredness, and Dark-Brownish Urine

RELATED SYMPTOMS: The dog may have a fever and her skin, gums, and tongue may be yellow-tinged. She may lose weight and have no interest in food, but may be excessively thirsty. The abdomen may appear bloated and the animal may stagger and experience seizures.

POSSIBLE CAUSES: Does your dog pal around with neighborhood pooches? Could she have ingested poisonous materials (including garden pesticides or household chemicals) or picked up a blood parasite when not under your supervision? Is she taking one or more types of oral medication? Does she have heart disease, diabetes, or cancer? Has she ever experienced starvation? Is she extremely overweight and/or eating a high-fat diet? A "yes" to any of these dissimilar questions may indicate a **liver disease,** including **acute hepatitis** (also known as infectious hepatitis), **chronic hepatitis,** or a **tumor in the liver.**

The liver filters all toxins from the blood and converts carbohydrates, proteins, and fats into nutrients for the body's use. When asked to work overtime—for instance, when an overload of toxic substances, medications, or fat must be cleansed from the blood—the liver can become damaged and enlarged. As in the case of acute or infectious hepatitis, the dog can actually catch a liver disease from a canine pal.

CARE: Take your dog to the vet, who will use any of the following tools to reach a diagnosis: a radiographic exam to highlight an enlarged or shrunken liver, blood tests to uncover an unnaturally high number of liver enzymes, a liver function test, or even a biopsy.

Fortunately, most livers can regenerate themselves after injury. Thus, your vet will concentrate on eliminating the underlying cause so the organ can heal. Your dog must strictly follow a low-protein, low-fat, easily digestible diet and—depending on the condition and what caused it—may be placed on antibiotics, diuretics, and/or steroids. Nutritional support in the form of vitamins, enzymes, and antioxidants is most valuable.

Other things you can do to treat your dog's liver disease at home at include giving her an amino-acid mix containing cysteine, glutathione, and methionine to protect the liver and encourage toxification. Milk thistle and dandelion are herbs frequently used to treat liver disease. Yeast-free vitamin B and vitamins C and E are also recommended (see Appendix E, List of Recommended Dosages, pp. 200–223).

PREVENTION: Feed your dog a low-protein/low-fat diet and closely supervise her play. To avoid undue stress to the liver, promptly attend to any illness. Vaccinate your dog against infectious hepatitis.

Vomiting, High Fever, Rapid Breathing, Arched Back, and Cautious Movements

RELATED SYMPTOMS: The dog will be weak, her pulse will be racing, and she will have severe abdominal pain that makes her ease into a lying down position.

POSSIBLE CAUSE: Could your dog have swallowed a foreign object? Has she recently been injured? Was she recently diagnosed with a uterine infection or acute inflammation of the pancreas? A "yes" to one of these questions can indicate **peritonitis,** a severe condition marked by an inflammation and/or infection in the abdominal cavity.

The peritoneum is a smooth, transparent membrane that lines the abdomen, the cavity many organs call home—including the intestines, spleen, bladder, liver, stomach, prostate (in males), and pancreas. If one of these organs becomes injured or torn—due to illness, a lodged foreign object, or an injurious blow—this lining can react by becoming inflamed and infected, thus affecting the entire abdominal cavity.

CARE: Peritonitis leads to death. **Take your dog immediately to the vet,** who will physically examine the animal as well as perform blood tests, urine analysis, and X rays. Should your pooch have peritonitis, your vet will treat her with high doses of antibiotics and anti-inflammatory medication before actually opening the animal up surgically to explore the abdomen, drain the area, and correct a tear if one exists. Follow-up care consists of 1 or 2 weeks of antibiotics, and giving your dog antioxidant vitamins and minerals (recommended by your vet) to support the immune system is advised.

PREVENTION: Supervise your dog's playtime to prevent her from swallowing foreign objects or being hit by a car or bike. Prevent your dog from getting into the garbage, which can have fatty food that can also stimulate pancreatitis. Have your female dog spayed so she will not develop a pus-filled uterus that can rupture into the abdomen.

CHAPTER 9

Spine, Limbs, and Paws

Dogs are usually thought of as active, playful crea- tures—animals who are always ready for a game of catch or a quick run. Yet, in order to lead such an action-packed life, your pooch needs strong, resilient muscles for smooth movement and hardy bones to support her weight, cushion the impact of all this verve, and protect her innards.

Though a number of ailments can affect the mus- culoskeletal system—from cancer to bone fractures to muscle sprains—most produce locomotive symp- toms. Such signals are usually easy to pick up on. After all, when a dog can't—or won't—move, or be- gins carrying himself in an unusual way, his loving owner can't help but notice.

Change in Posture and Paralysis

Many things can cause a change in your pet's posture: An energy-sapping illness like pneumonia will make it hard for a weakened dog to stand up straight; an injury can alter a pooch's carriage depending on what hurts; any ailment affecting an abdominal organ can leave an animal hunched- up in pain; and so on. The important thing is to note what symptoms are accompanying the change in posture. How- ever, in cases where altered posture is the primary symp- tom, a **vertebral** or **spinal condition** is more often to blame.

Your dog can't move a body part at all? Vets refer to this as **paralysis**, and it can affect the neck, a leg, two legs, all legs, the tail, the spine, or a combination of body parts.

Causes include **traumatic nerve damage** (i.e., from a broken bone), a **herniated disc**, a **brain** or **spinal tumor**, or other **nervous-system disorders**. It may even be an inherited ailment. Should you notice that your pooch is unable to move a body part, you may find other signs that something is wrong, such as pain, changes in eating or elimination habits, and swollen areas. Make a note of these and visit your vet, who will be able to make a diagnosis. (Also see section in Chapter 3, Frozen Facial Muscles, Stiff Gait, and Difficulty Moving Limbs, Neck, and Head, p. 26).

Paralysis of the Face

RELATED SYMPTOMS: The dog's eyes, eyelids, ears, nostrils, and/or lips are not moving. Either one side or both sides of the face will be affected. Your dog may be messier than usual while eating and may drool. The dog might rub his eyes, his eyelids may not shut, and there may be discharge oozing from the eyes.

POSSIBLE CAUSE: Is your dog an adult cocker spaniel, Welsh corgi, boxer, or English setter? Has your pet recently been diagnosed with an ear condition or involved in an accident that resulted in some type of facial trauma? A "yes" to either question may indicate **facial nerve paralysis**, an ailment where the facial nerve becomes impaired, making facial movements difficult. The condition is genetic in some dog breeds, but it can also affect any pooch suffering from trauma or an illness affecting the head.

CARE: Take your pooch to the vet, who will diagnose the condition after performing a physical and neurologic exam and perhaps take radiographs. Treatment will depend on the cause of the paralysis.

PREVENTION: Although there's little you can do for breeds predisposed to the condition, you can prevent facial nerve paralysis in other breeds by addressing ear, mouth, nose, and eye conditions promptly. Also, supervise outdoor play to keep dogs from being involved in accidents.

Rigid or Flaccid Paralysis of the Front Legs or the Hindquarters, Cries of Pain When Picked Up or Petted Along the Spine, and Active Avoidance of Stairs and Jumping

RELATED SYMPTOMS: Depending on the severity of the problem, your dog may knuckle over when he walks, his back end may sway in a "drunken" manner, or he may be fully or partially paralyzed in any or all of his limbs. If a cervical (neck) disc is the culprit, bending his neck may result in severe pain.

POSSIBLE CAUSE: Is yours a dog with a long back and short legs such as a dachshund, basset hound, Welsh corgi, toy poodle, Pekingese, shih tzu, French bulldog, Lhasa apso, beagle, a type of spaniel or schnauzer, or a mix of any of these breeds? Is he older than five years? He may have a **herniated disc**, also known as a **ruptured** or **prolapsed disc** or **intervertebral disc disease**. This is a traumatic or hereditary condition where the outside covering of the disc becomes weak and eventually ruptures. When the thick, cartilogenous covering of the disc ruptures, the gelatinous center of the disc leaks out and moves into spots where it puts painful pressure on the spinal cord or roots of the spinal nerves. It should be noted that this condition can affect discs anywhere along the spine, from the base of the neck to the pelvis.

CARE: If the condition has dramatically worsened over the course of 2 to 3 days, **take your pooch to the vet immediately**. If possible, carry him in a pet carrier or other container with a hard, flat surface so that his spine isn't subject to movement. If the dog can walk and the condition has stayed constant for weeks, the circumstances aren't as dire. Yes, your pet will need to see a vet for a diagnosis, but it isn't an emergency: You can schedule an appointment for the following week and still be okay. In either case, the vet will perform a physical exam and take radiographs or a myelogram to determine the location of the affected discs.

Milder cases require nothing more than veterinary physiotherapy, which consists of whirlpool baths, swimming, passive joint exercise, and the application of heat (via a hot-water bottle or heat lamp) to the affected region. A heating pad applied to the most sensitive area of the back 3 times a day can make your dog more comfortable. You can also give your dog buffered aspirin for relief (¼ of a 325-mg tablet or an 81-mg baby aspirin for every 10 pounds of body weight). Since pain is nature's way of preventing your pooch from overworking a damaged joint (thus possibly injuring it further), many vets are hesitant to administer pain medication. However, cortisone therapy may be advised to help take the pressure off affected nerves. (However, cortisone and aspirin should never be given to your dog at the same time; the combination could lead to gastric or intestinal ulceration.) In severe cases, surgery will be performed to remove the ruptured or protruding disc (or discs) and take pressure off the affected spinal cord or nerve roots.

Whether your dog has undergone surgery or been diagnosed with a less serious disc problem, certain homecare measures can make your pet more comfortable. Feed him a concentrated proteolytic enzyme (available at health-food stores) 3 or 4 times a day, and give him vitamin E (200 to 800 IU depending on his size). Vitamin C, chondroitin sulfate, and glucosamine sulfate can help strengthen the connective tissue of the joint (see Appendix E, List of Recommended Dosages, pp. 200–223). If you have stairs, don't allow your dog to use them—carry the pooch up and down steps when necessary. Likewise, don't allow your pet to jump on or off anything elevated, including furniture. If you are used to active play and/or roughhousing with your pet, stop this interaction until the dog is well. Actually, **the equivalent to human bed rest is the best advice** for a dog suffering from a herniated disc. Sometimes, "cage rest" is the best recommendation.

PREVENTION: Although intervertebral disc disease cannot be totally prevented, keeping your dog at a healthy weight for his frame will make him more comfortable and less likely to develop a herniated disc. If he is already over-weight, put him on a weight-reduction plan.

Severe Neck Pain, Bouts of Neck Rigidity, and Inactivity

RELATED SYMPTOMS: Each bout usually lasts 5 to 10 days, during which time the dog may appear depressed and have a fever. Following this, a period of relative normalcy lasts from 1 to 3 weeks. Then the cycle starts again with another bout.

POSSIBLE CAUSE: Is your dog a young beagle, boxer, German shorthaired pointer, Akita, or Bernese mountain dog? He may have **immune-mediated meningitis**, an inflammation of the membranes that line the brain and spinal cord. The underlying cause is unknown. Also unknown is why these breeds seem predisposed to the condition. After 2 to 5 months of this attack-normalcy cycle, the ailment usually disappears by itself.

CARE: Take your dog to the vet, who will run blood tests to reach a diagnosis. Cortisone therapy can minimize the severity of an attack by reducing the inflammation of the affected brain and spinal-cord membranes. You can help to boost your dog's immune system by feeding him a high-quality, chemical-free diet and vitamin C administered 6 times a day and dosed to bowel tolerance (when the stool begins to get loose, cut the dose back just enough to obtain a normal stool) (see Appendix E, List of Recommended Dosages, pp. 200–223).

PREVENTION: Because it is not known what causes the condition, immune-mediated meningitis is difficult to prevent.

Lameness

In vet-speak, **lameness** refers to any leg (or legs) that a dog is unable or unwilling to use in a normal fashion. With severe lameness, the dog will either hold his leg off the ground or literally drag the limb on the ground. With mild lameness, the gait may look almost normal, but on close inspection, the dog may "favor" the limb by putting less weight on it or bearing weight on it for a shorter time.

The reason a dog can't or won't put his weight on a limb isn't always a serious one. In fact, should you notice your dog suddenly avoiding using a leg, check the connecting paw. Quite often a **sharp object is stuck in the footpad**, making it uncomfortable to bear weight on the leg. Other reasons for not using a foot include **puncture wounds, cuts**, or **abrasions**. A **cracked toenail** may also be a cause (as minor as it sounds, a broken claw can cause your dog much pain). A sprain or strain to muscles, ligaments, or tendons of the leg—due to overexercise or an accident—will also keep a dog off his limb. Torn ligaments, especially of the knee joint, are another common cause of lameness, as is damage or disease of the joint cartilage.

If the lameness has come on more slowly, there may be a more serious underlying medical cause, such as a **fracture** or **bone cancer**. In a young puppy, lameness can indicate that some of the **limb bones are growing irregularly**, whereas in a mature pooch, lameness is often brought on by **arthritis**. Lameness may also result from an **injury to the spinal cord** or **to the nerves** going to the leg muscles. [Also see sections in Chapter 3, Wobbliness When Standing or Walking and Incoordination of Limbs pp. 28–29, and Swollen Lymph Nodes, Fever, Painful Joints (i.e., Lameness), and Neurological Abnormalities, p. 34.]

Intermittent or Constant Lameness in One or Both Front Legs; May Alternate with Periods When Walking with Elbow Held Out and Is Reluctant to Bear Weight on Affected Leg(s)

RELATED SYMPTOMS: The symptoms will become noticeably worse after your dog rises from a reclining position, exercises, walks down a hill, or descends steps. You may also notice thickening of the elbow joint on the affected leg(s).

POSSIBLE CAUSE: Is your pooch a dachshund or a large to giant breed or giant-breed mix? Is he younger than a year old? He may have **elbow dysplasia**, an inherited disease that causes elbow joints to develop abnormally. Because of this abnormal development, the joints are unstable, painful, and cannot distribute the dog's weight properly.

CARE: Your vet can usually diagnose the disease after taking an X ray. Medical measures to treat elbow dysplasia include a bone-cutting procedure that creates a more normal, stable elbow in a developing animal. In severe cases, elbow-replacement surgery may be performed.

PREVENTION: If your puppy is of a large breed or large-breed mix or is a dachshund, have him X-rayed for the detection of elbow dysplasia, thus allowing early treatment if needed. In predisposed dogs of all ages, vigorously maintain normal body weight. This will not prevent elbow dysplasia, but it can prevent a mild case from becoming severe.

Lameness in One Hind Leg

RELATED SYMPTOMS: You may notice the dog dragging a hind leg or walking with a hop.

POSSIBLE CAUSES: Is your dog between five and ten months old? Is he a small breed or breed mix? There's a chance he has a congenital deformity of the femur head (the "ball") and neck, medically referred to as a **necrosis of the femoral head and neck**. The condition is caused when the blood supply to the head and neck of the developing femur is damaged and the normally ball-shaped femoral head takes on a less than round appearance. Breeders' tendencies to produce increasingly small dogs is a contributing factor to the ailment.

CARE: Take your dog to the vet, who can diagnose the condition after performing a radiograph exam. Should your dog have a deformed femur head, the only solution is arthroplasty. In this procedure, the malformed portion of the bone is removed and the connective tissue between the pelvis and the femur form a substitute (or "false") joint. The sutures will be removed after 10 days, and the dog should be walking relatively normally within 1 month. A much more sophisticated and expensive operation exists that actually replaces the damaged head with a prosthetic ball.

Supplementing your dog's diet with vitamins C and E and selenium can help to reduce pain and inflammation, and glucosamine sulfate and chondroitin sulfate are useful in increasing the lubricating properties of the joint fluid (see Appendix E, List of Recommended Dosages, pp. 200–223).

PREVENTION: Because this is a congenital defect, there is no prevention. Dogs with this condition, however, should not be allowed to produce offspring due to the chance of passing the ailment on to the following generation. Therefore neutering is advised.

Lameness in One Leg, Swelling and Obvious Painfulness, and Noticeable Warmth in a Localized Spot of Leg Bone

RELATED SYMPTOMS: The dog will have a fever and the affected area may also develop a deep, oozing wound.

POSSIBLE CAUSE: Was your pet recently bitten by another dog or wild animal? Has he undergone any type of surgery lately? Did he recently recover from an infection to an internal organ, blood, or the skin? A "yes" to any of these may indicate a bone infection, known medically as **osteomyelitis**. Just like skin, bone can also become infected. Although animal bites and contaminated surgery are often to blame, an infection in another area of the body could have spread to the bone via the bloodstream. Regardless of the cause, a bone infection can work its way up through the skin, resulting in deep, pus-draining sores.

CARE: Take your pooch to the vet, who will perform a physical examination and take an X ray. A bacterial culture of any material seeping from the site helps identify the organism responsible for the infection, thus making it easier to select an effective antibiotic. In addition to antibiotic therapy, surgery is sometimes necessary to remove bony fragments and debris and establish better drainage. You can also give your dog high levels of proteolytic enzymes and dimethylglycine (both found in health-food stores) to help the dog's immune system destroy the bacterial infection in the bone (see Appendix E, List of Recommended Dosages, pp. 200–223).

PREVENTION: Supervise your dog's play and attend to any wounds immediately.

Lameness in One or Both Rear Legs and Difficulty in Getting Up and Lying Down

RELATED SYMPTOMS: The dog has a swaying or wad-dling walk and may appear knock-kneed. Due to his diffi-culty in moving, the animal may appear lazy. If he can still run, he may appear to run "like a rabbit," with both hind legs moving together.

POSSIBLE CAUSE: Is yours a large, heavy dog? He may have **hip dysplasia**, a partially hereditary disease of the hip joint that affects mainly large breeds of dogs. The condition begins as a dog is growing, caused when the hip joint de-velops improperly and results in a loose-fitting and mal-formed ball-and-socket joint. Hip dysplasia is made worse by excessive use and eventually develops into arthritis.

CARE: Hip dysplasia is not curable. If yours is an adult pooch, is not in severe pain, and the condition is not de-teriorating, there are things you can do at home to make your pet more comfortable: Don't let your dog jump or exercise heavily, keep the environment warm and dry, don't allow the animal to become overweight (extra weight stresses the hip joints).

As for diagnosing hip dysplasia, visit the vet. Only an X ray can make a definite diagnosis. A dog who is still growing definitely should be seen by a vet. For many pup-pies, a simple operation that severs a muscle on the inside of the thigh helps relieve pain. Also, many vets have suc-cess with corrective osteotomy done between six and ten months of age. This is a bone-cutting procedure that creates a more normal, stable hip in a developing animal.

For adult dogs with advanced hip dysplasia who are in severe, constant pain, total hip replacement is an option that allows them to walk with little apparent pain or difficulty. Nonsurgical options include painkillers given whenever the pain becomes severe. Ask your vet about acupuncture to relieve discomfort. The use of nutritional antioxidant supplements and glucosamine sulfate and chondroitin sulfate are together very helpful in treating the condition and reducing joint pain. You can also give your dog the antioxidants vitamin E (200 to 400 IU daily) and vitamin C (given to bowel tolerance 3 times a day) to relieve pain and inflammation, strengthen ligaments and connective tissue surrounding the joint, and slow the disease's progression (see Appendix E, List of Recommended Dosages, pp. 200–223).

PREVENTION: If your puppy is of a large breed or large-breed mix, have him X-rayed for the detection of hip dysplasia, thus allowing early treatment if needed. For large dogs of all ages, prevent abnormal weight gain (obesity). This will not prevent hip dysplasia, but it may prevent a mild case from becoming severe. There are veterinary nutritionists who believe that young, rapidly growing pups should, at some point in their growth, be placed on a reduced protein diet in an attempt to slow the rate of growth and reduce the likelihood of hip dysplasia developing. Consult your vet.

Lameness in One or More Legs and Broken Nails on Affected Paws

RELATED SYMPTOM: The broken toenails will still be partially connected to the paw.

POSSIBLE CAUSE: Do you clip your dog's toenails infrequently, if at all? There's a chance one or more **nails are broken**—an uncomfortable situation where a claw hangs by just a thread of connective nail. This is one of those minor conditions that can cause severe enough pain to keep a dog off his affected feet.

CARE: If there are no infected areas (i.e., if the adjoining toe is not severely swollen), this is something you can try to take care of yourself. The condition can be very painful if the nerve is exposed, so be sure to muzzle the dog before proceeding. It's helpful to have someone hold the dog, petting him and keeping him calm (and distracted). If the nail is hanging by a thread, take a pair of needle-nosed pliers or tweezers (or you can use your fingers) and give a quick, hard tug and twist at the *end* of a cracked, broken toenail. If the broken nail is more completely attached, a nail cutter may be a better instrument to use. Your pooch probably won't like this, but the broken end needs to come off. There may be light to moderate bleeding that can be stopped by placing a bandage against the area and applying pressure for 3 to 5 minutes or bandaging the foot for several hours. If the broken nail is cracked but still quite closely attached, I recommend you visit your vet. Cutting off the broken end of such a nail fracture can cause more bleeding than you may be comfortable with, so let the vet handle it.

PREVENTION: Because overgrown toenails are most likely to break, keep your dog's nails trimmed. (See Appendix A, Checklist for Good Health, pp. 178–185.)

Lameness, Pain When Walking, and Thick-Looking Joints

RELATED SYMPTOMS: One or more limbs may be affected. Lameness may be mild, moderate, or severe and is especially prevalent after exercise.

POSSIBLE CAUSE: Is yours a large or giant-breed dog, such as a Great Dane, Labrador retriever, Newfoundland, rottweiler, Bernese mountain dog, English setter, or Old English sheepdog? Is he between four and eighteen months of age? Your pet may have **osteochondrosis**, a hereditary condition where the joint cartilage does not develop properly.

CARE: Take your pet to the vet, who will perform a physical exam, radiograph, and/or MRI to diagnose the condition. Treatment includes weight reducing for obese animals and limiting exercise in order to reduce stress on joints. If the condition becomes severe, surgery may be indicated.

PREVENTION: None. Avoid breeding dogs who have osteochondrosis.

Lameness That May Shift from One or Both Forelimbs to One or Both Hind Legs, Accompanied by Mild Depression

RELATED SYMPTOMS: The dog may or may not "carry" the affected leg. He may also lose his appetite and lose weight. Pressing on the long bones of the legs may produce a painful response.

POSSIBLE CAUSE: Is yours a male, medium to large-breed dog, aged five months to five years? He may have **panosteitis**, a condition characterized by higher-than-usual bone-marrow density. The actual cause of this condition is unknown.

CARE: Take your dog to the vet who will perform a radiograph to determine the presence of panosteitis. Treatment includes reduced exercise and anti-inflammatory medicine.

PREVENTION: There is no known prevention.

Limping on One Leg and Licking Affected Paw

RELATED SYMPTOMS: You may notice small smears of blood on the floor where your dog sets down the affected paw.

POSSIBLE CAUSE: Could your dog have stepped on a sharp piece of glass, a thorn, or other sharp material during an unsupervised moment? There's a chance he may have a **cut** or **puncture wound on his footpad.** This is easily determined by simply looking carefully at the bottom of your dog's foot and in between the pads.

CARE: If the cut is a deep one, your goal is to prevent severe blood loss. Immediately press a towel or bandage to the area and apply pressure or a pressure bandage until the bleeding stops. Continue to hold the compress in place as you take your pet to the vet (you may need a second person for this). A cut that requires pressure to stop the blood flow often also requires stitches.

If bleeding is minimal, examine the area for foreign material. If the footpad is object-free, wash it with antibacterial soap and water, rinse and dry thoroughly, and wrap the paw with a gauze bandage to keep it clean and speed healing.

If something is embedded in the flesh, you can try to remove it. Start by muzzling your dog: Even the gentlest canine can get scared enough to nip at you. After all, he doesn't know what you're doing with those tweezers—only that you're messing with a foot that already hurts! If the object can be easily removed with tweezers, quickly yank it out. If it is embedded too deeply, you may need to coax the object to the surface with a sterilized sewing needle or straight pin, much like you would when removing an embedded splinter in your own hand. Once the intruder is at the surface, you can use your tweezers to pull it out. Finish by washing the area with soap and water, flushing it with 3% hydrogen peroxide, drying it, and wrapping a gauze bandage around the paw. Any bleeding should stop within 5 minutes and the dog should be putting pressure on the foot within 2 to 3 hours. If you haven't removed the entire object, if the animal doesn't put pressure on his foot after a few hours, or if an infection sets in within the next 48 hours, take your pooch to the vet.

PREVENTION: Supervise your dog's playtime and attempt to keep dangerous objects off the ground and away from your dog's exercise area.

Limping on One or More Legs and a Raw-Looking Footpad on Affected Paw

RELATED SYMPTOMS: When you examine the footpad of the leg your dog is limping on, you may also notice blisters, cuts, or flaps of hanging skin. The dog may lick affected paws.

POSSIBLE CAUSE: Has your dog been walking on salt-treated surfaces (in winter) or hot asphalt (in summer)? Has your pet been traversing rough, rocky terrain? Has your pet been running for longer-than-usual periods on any hard surface? A "yes" to any of these may point to **footpad abrasion.** The condition is caused when the tough, protective skin of the footpad is worn away, exposing the tender tissue beneath.

CARE: If infection has set in (indicated by the presence of oozing pus), take your dog to the vet. Otherwise, if the abrasions are not too severe, this is something you can treat at home. Wash the area with warm water and mild antibacterial soap, rinse, then thoroughly dry it. Next, swab the footpad with an antiseptic solution, such as chlorhexidine or iodine. An antibiotic ointment, such as bacitracin, can be applied to particularly raw spots to ward off infection. You can attempt to seal a superficial abrasion (thus reducing pain and protecting the wound from further contamination) by using a product such as New Skin, or tincture of benzoin (but be aware that these substances may momentarily sting your dog). After the sealing substance dries, bandage the paw.

Try to keep your dog's exercise to a minimum during the healing process. This can take up to 2 weeks. If your pooch must be on his feet (or refuses to stay still), heavily bandage the paws to keep them from directly contacting the ground.

PREVENTION: Avoid walking your dog on hot asphalt or salted sidewalks. Avoid excessive long jogs on hard surfaces. Should your pooch's paws come in contact with salt (which dries and irritates the skin and causes it to crack), manually remove the salt granules and wash them with water and mild soap. Rinse well and dry thoroughly. If yours is an active dog, encourage him to run on grassy areas or take him to a park for exercise.

Limping, Swelling, and Tenderness in One Leg

RELATED SYMPTOMS: A mild limp may progress into a total nonweight-bearing leg.

POSSIBLE CAUSE: Is yours a large or giant breed or breed mix? There's a chance he has a **bone tumor.**

CARE: Unfortunately, the majority of skeletal tumors are malignant. Take your dog to the vet, who will perform a radiographic exam to determine the presence of a tumor. A biopsy of the tumor can determine whether it is benign or malignant. Bone tumors very infrequently are benign, but in such a situation, I would advise leaving it alone after the diagnosis is made.

If the growth is malignant, your vet will remove the affected bone as quickly as possible—this usually involves amputating a portion of a limb. If two or more tumors are found on a leg, the entire limb may be amputated. Though this sounds extreme, most dogs adapt well to three-legged life. To prevent the cancer from showing up in another body site, it is common practice to follow tumor removal and/or amputation with chemotherapy. (Chest X rays will be taken before surgery to determine whether the tumor has spread to the lungs.)

PREVENTION: Nothing can be done to prevent bone cancer other than maintaining a healthy body and a strong immune system.

Mild to Severe Lameness in Hind and/or Front Legs Upon Rising, Thickening of the Joints of Affected Legs, Overall Stiffness, and Apathy

RELATED SYMPTOMS: Although it doesn't disappear, the lameness improves after the dog has taken part in mild exercise. If you gently move the affected joints, you may hear a grinding noise of bone grating against cartilage and/or bone. You may notice the presence of a mild fever that seems to randomly appear, disappear, and reappear. These symptoms may have developed slowly over the course of several years.

POSSIBLE CAUSE: Has your dog experienced a joint injury or infection at any time in the past? Is he a mature animal? Is he a larger member of a working or sporting breed (such as any type of retriever or shepherd) or a toy breed (such as one of the smaller poodles or terriers)? A "yes" to one or more of these questions may indicate a type of **arthritis**, which simply means **joint inflammation.** The disease has causes, including old age or previous trauma to a joint due to infection or injury. In the case of congenital arthritis, some breeds are genetically predisposed to getting arthritis. Immune-system diseases may also result in arthritis.

CARE: If you're unsure your pooch has arthritis—or if your dog's lameness is severe—visit your vet, who will perform a physical exam and take X rays. In moderate to moderately severe cases, your vet may prescribe anti-inflammatory pain medication such as NSAIDs (nonsteroidal anti-inflammatory drugs) and nutritional supplements such as antioxidants, glucosamine sulfate, chondroitin sulfate, and methylsulfonyl methane, which both suppress inflammation and help the body repair damage already done to the joint cartilage and joint fluid. In dogs predisposed toward arthritis, these remedies may need to be continued for life. Try to avoid the use of steroid/cortisone medications that, though excellent at reducing pain and inflammation, may eventually result in negative side effects.

In more severe cases, loose cartilage may be present in the joint. If so, your veterinarian will surgically remove the detached matter. Should the joint be so painful that moving it causes your dog to suffer, your vet may, when possible, opt for an operation to immobilize the joint, rendering it unmovable. This last procedure is typically done to only one joint and, since the remaining joints remain mobile, it doesn't severely impair walking.

If the arthritis is mild, there are easy homecare measures you can employ that will make the dog more comfortable. First, since extra weight taxes the joints, it is essential that an arthritic, overweight dog thins down. Also, keep the environment warm; cold air makes joints stiff and achy. Vitamins C and E and selenium are extremely helpful antioxidants and anti-inflammatory agents (see Appendix E,

List of Recommended Dosages, pp. 200–223).

Moderate exercise—and the operative word here is moderate—is an essential part of homecare. (No frisbee-catching, stick-fetching, or runs in the park!) If you and your pooch are used to taking one 60-minute daily walk, consider breaking it into three 20-minute walks, four 15-minute walks, or six 10-minute walks. And last but not least, instead of allowing your dog to sleep on hard surfaces, provide soft bedding for comfort's sake.

PREVENTION: You can't prevent arthritis in a dog genetically inclined to the condition, but you can ward off the ailment in a nondisposed animal by helping him avoid joint injuries, such as those a dog may get when hit by a car. In many larger breeds, arthritis can become so severe that the dog cannot get up, and euthanasia may need to be performed: Therefore, it is very important to prevent the progressive worsening of this condition. Again, antioxidants vitamins C and E and supplements glucosamine sulfate and chondroitin sulfate may greatly slow down progressive joint disease (see Appendix E, List of Recommended Dosages, pp. 200–223).

Mild to Severe Lameness in One Leg, Possibly the Result of an Acute Injury

RELATED SYMPTOMS: Your dog will have difficulty walking. His gait may be just slightly impaired or the dog may actually carry the limb.

POSSIBLE CAUSE: Is yours a large breed dog under the age of two? Is he a middle-aged dog of any breed type? Is your pet overweight? Has he been in an accident recently? He may have **cruciate disease**, a condition characterized by injury to the cruciate ligament due to genetic weakness, obesity, or trauma. The cruciate ligament is the ligament in the center of the knee joint that stabilizes and prevents abnormal movement.

CARE: Take your pet to the vet, who will perform a physical exam and perhaps take an X ray to diagnose the condition. Since obesity exacerbates the condition, if the dog is overweight, he will be put on a diet. You can also give your pet supplements such as vitamins C and E and shark cartilage (see Appendix E, List of Recommended Dosages, pp. 200–223) to strengthen the connective tissue surrounding the knee, enabling it to compensate for the cruciate ligament. Although the cruciate ligament will not regrow, surgery to replace the damaged ligament is successful in some animals.

PREVENTION: Keep your dog from becoming overweight, and keep him away from icy or slippery areas.

Weakness and Lack of Coordination in the Hind Legs

RELATED SYMPTOMS: The animal may shuffle his feet or "knuckle over" when walking. He may have lost control over his bowels and bladder. It may be difficult for the dog to rise or ascend stairs. His back end may sway in a "drunken" manner when walking.

POSSIBLE CAUSE: Is your dog a middle-aged German shepherd, Siberian husky, collie, Labrador retriever, Chesapeake Bay retriever, Kerry blue terrier, or a medium- to large-sized mix of any of the breeds just mentioned? It is possible your dog has **degenerative myelopathy,** a disease characterized by the slow degeneration of the spinal cord.

CARE: Take your pet to the vet, who will take radiographs of the animal's spine in order to rule out other diseases that have similar symptoms (such as degenerative disk disease). There is no effective treatment for this disease, but your vet will counsel you on homecare. Typically, she recommends daily exercise to keep your dog strong and a reduction diet (if he is overweight). A high-quality chemical-free diet is advised and vitamins C and E should also be tried (see Appendix E, List of Recommended Dosages, pp. 200–223).

PREVENTION: There is no prevention.

Stiff or Unusual Movements

Falling over, trembling, stiff legs, a disjointed gait—all

are admittedly upsetting signs. When in the presence of ailments such as distemper, heart disease, tumors, or poisoning, these often accompany other symptoms, such as coughing, vomiting, or fever. Yet, when these **symptoms of incoordination** come on quickly and are the only ones present, it's wise to visit your vet immediately.

Skipping and Frequent Lifting of One or Both Hind Legs

RELATED SYMPTOMS: If both legs are affected, the dog will hop with a rounded back like a rabbit. You may notice thickening of the affected knee joint (or joints).

POSSIBLE CAUSE: Is yours a small dog between the ages of four months and a year? He may be suffering from a **slipping kneecap**. This condition, also called **luxating patella,** usually appears first when the dog is young. It's a common hereditary deformity of the knee joints that strikes small dogs. Due to the malformation of the bones forming the knee joint, the kneecap slips, either inward or outward, out of its normal position in the joint. Depending on the severity of the deformity, the kneecap may slip in and out of place intermittently or move out of place permanently.

CARE: Very mild cases cause only mild intermittent lameness and do not require treatment, although it is wise to take your dog to the vet to get a professional confirming diagnosis. In more severe cases, which cause serious lameness, your vet can surgically reconstruct the knee joint and stabilize the knee cap, allowing your dog near-normal movement. To help strengthen the connective tissue surrounding the knee joint and repair injury to the cartilage of the knee, give your dog vitamin C and chondroitin sulfate and glucosamine sulfate (see Appendix E, List of Recommended Dosages, pp. 200–223).

PREVENTION: There is no prevention. If you want a small dog, ask a vet to help you choose a healthy, sound animal. Having a vet inspect an animal before you decide to keep him can help ensure that you don't unknowingly select a pooch with this problem. To avoid "creating" pups with this condition, dogs with slipping kneecaps should not be allowed to breed. Therefore neutering is advised.

Stiff-Legged Gait, Incoordination, Weakness, Muscles That Appear Frozen, and Convulsions

SYMPTOMS: The dog's ears will be frozen in an erect stance, his mouth drawn back (almost appearing to grin), and his eyes narrowed. He will have difficulty swallowing and may be drooling. You may see vertical lines on his forehead. The dog may have a fever.

POSSIBLE CAUSE: Did your dog receive some type of deep puncture wound in the last 48 hours? If so, there's a chance he has **tetanus**. The condition is caused by bacteria that enter the body through a puncture wound. These bacteria release a nerve toxin that causes the body's muscles to stiffen.

CARE: Take your dog immediately to the vet, who will quickly administer tetanus antiserum and antibiotics. To help further relax frozen muscles, strong sedatives will be given. Because 1 to 2 weeks of rest helps the dog's chances of recovery, narcotics may also be given. Be aware, however, that tetanus can be fatal to dogs, even when veterinary care has been given.

PREVENTION: Supervise your dog's play. Canines are highly resistant to the bacterium that causes tetanus (much more so than humans are) so they rarely develop the condition and are rarely vaccinated for it. But if you live in an area with livestock, talk to your vet about a tetanus shot, because the tetanus-causing bacterium thrives in manure and manure-contaminated soil.

CHAPTER 10

Tail and Anus

When most of us think of our dog's back end—if we think of it at all—the tail is probably the first thing that comes to mind. Yet, that's not all there is to your pooch's posterior. It's wise to pay attention to the anus, too—it's an excellent harbinger of your pup's overall wellness.

Yes, this particular body part has an unsavory reputation, which is unfortunate. The anus works hard to finish off the digestive process started by the mouth and stomach. A change in anything leaving the anus can indicate the start of an overall health problem that can be caught and addressed while still minor. Changes in feces can also hint to a more major ailment involving the intestines, prostate, or internal area. Of course, the backside can be plagued by a few illnesses that strike solely this area, such as prolapsed rectum or blocked anal glands. By keeping a careful watch on your dog's behavior and appearance, you'll know when there's a problem.

Conditions of the Tail and Anal Region

Wondering what kind of mood your dog is in? Look at her tail: High in the air and she's ready to play; tucked between her legs and she's feeling scared; wagging and she's thrilled to see you. We humans place such importance on a dog's tail movements that to see the appendage stuck in one position can be scary. Yet injury to one or more of the tail's vertebrae or to the region where the tail joins the pelvis can do just that, freezing the tail in a limp position between the legs.

You may, however, notice something is wrong with another part of your pooch's backside: the anus. If you catch your dog repeatedly sniffing or licking the area or scooting it along the ground, you can be pretty sure that something's bothering your pet. This something could have a nonmedical cause, such as your dog sitting on something sticky, not cleaning herself thoroughly after eliminating, or not getting all the soap rinsed off after a bath. Since longhaired dogs are especially susceptible to these irritating situations, it helps to keep the fur around the backside clipped short. This will prevent anal secretions and bits of feces from becoming embedded, which smells bad and also makes your dog itch.

Unfortunately, such behavior can also indicate a health condition that directly targets the anus and anal glands, such as an **impaction**, **abscess**, or **tumor.**

Bent-Looking or Limp Tail That Doesn't Move

RELATED SYMPTOMS: The dog may yelp when her tail is touched or may shrink from being petted on her backside.

POSSIBLE CAUSES: Does your dog play outside unsupervised? Was she recently in an accident or in a fight with another dog? Did she have her tail slammed in a door? Your pooch's **tail may be fractured, dislocated,** or **bruised.** There may be an **injury to the nerves** that go to the muscles of the tail, which can produce paralysis.

CARE: Take your pet to the vet. Because animals suffering from broken bones often bite out of pain and fear, muzzle your dog to keep her from wounding you, your vet, or your vet's assistant. An X ray can confirm whether any bones have been broken, fractured, or dislocated. If so, the tail will be set and bandaged around a splint.

A wound, either from a bite or cut, will be cleaned, medicated, and bandaged or stitched if necessary. Should your pooch suffer from a severe bruise, your vet will suggest that you keep the animal calm and comfortable indoors for 2 weeks so that the injury can heal. Injuries causing a tail paralysis will hopefully heal with time. If not, the tail may require amputation.

PREVENTION: Supervise your dog's play.

Injury to the Tip of the Tail, Accompanied by Bleeding

RELATED SYMPTOMS: The wound doesn't heal, even when you try to bandage the area. The skin may be abraded, and you may be able to see underlying muscle and/or bone.

POSSIBLE CAUSE: Has someone accidentally slammed your pooch's tail in a door or stepped on it? Could your dog have caught her tail in a gate, lawnmower, or some other sharp space during an unsupervised moment? The animal may have a **wound on the tip of her tail**. Unfortunately this is one area of a dog that is slow to heal and easily reinjured.

CARE: Take your dog to the vet. Anytime your dog wags her injured tail, she risks hitting the appendage on a nearby wall, the floor, or your leg. Wrapping the tip in a heavy layer of bandaging shields the wound, but if your dog is like most pooches, she probably will try to chew off this bandage. Thus, your vet will apply an Elizabethan collar, making it more difficult—but unfortunately not impossible—for your pet to reach around and nip her own tail.

PREVENTION: Keep your dog indoors when using a lawnmower or weed trimmer. Watch for your pet's tail when shutting house and car doors.

Puckered Skin Protruding from the Anus

RELATED SYMPTOMS: The dog may lick the area and you may notice her straining during defecation.

POSSIBLE CAUSE: Has your dog been straining to defecate lately? Has she been constipated? Does she eat a lot of bones? She may have a **prolapsed rectum.** The protruding puckered skin you see is actually an interior portion of the rectum that has been forced out through the anus, due to straining from attempts to pass bones and hard stool.

CARE: There are several things you can do at home to relieve your pet's constipation. Try feeding your dog raw meat (a natural laxative) or you can add powdered psyllium (such as Metamucil) to your dog's diet to keep the stool soft (see Appendix E, List of Recommended Dosages, pp. 200–223). You can also add ½ to 2 teaspoons of mineral oil mixed into the dog's food 2 times a day, for no more than 1 week, to relieve constipation. If your dog is still suffering from constipation, visit your vet, who may prescribe laxatives for severe conditions and will help you to design an easily digestible diet. Once your pooch starts voiding in a more normal fashion, the rectum can heal itself. Fecal softeners and laxatives may need to be given regularly or on an "as-needed" basis. If the rectum prolapses repeatedly, your vet can surgically suture the rectum to the abdominal wall.

PREVENTION: To prevent constipation, which, in turn, can lead to straining and rectal prolapse, encourage your pooch to drink generous amounts of water. Limit your dog's intake of bones.

Swollen Areas, Infected Sores, or Abscesses Around the Anus, Scooting the Anus Across the Ground, or Constant Licking of the Anus

RELATED SYMPTOMS: The area will often smell foul. Swelling around the rectum may be the only symptom, most noticeable at the "4 o'clock" and "8 o'clock" positions around the anus. More often infected sores or abscesses of the anal glands or perianal tissue are present, they may break open to reveal blood and pus, leaving a craterlike wound or a tunnel (known as a fistula).

POSSIBLE CAUSES: Is yours a mature male dog? Is he an unneutered dog? Is he a dog under 15 pounds? Is he a German Shepherd or Irish setter? A "yes" to any of these might indicate a condition concerning the anal glands or surrounding tissue—specifically **clogged anal glands, anal**

fistulas, an **anal gland abscess** (or **abscesses**), or an **anal tumor.**

To understand anal disorders, an anatomy lesson is in order: Anal glands, also called anal sacs and often referred to as "skunk glands," sit at the "4 o'clock" and "8 o'clock" positions just below the anus. They are lined with cells that manufacture an extremely foul-smelling liquid. As feces make their journey out of the anus, pressure is placed on these sacs, and they empty their stored material through tiny ducts located directly below and on either side of the anal opening. It's speculated that these sacs and their smelly secretions help dogs identify each other and mark territory, though no one has ever proven this.

If these anal sacs aren't emptied on a regular basis, the long-standing secretions thicken into a gummy, gritty sludge. Instead of a watery secretion that passes easily though the tiny duct, this pasty ooze gets stuck in the anal sacs—the problem is much like trying to squeeze toothpaste through a pinhole. This situation is especially dire for dogs weighing less than 15 pounds. Why? Smaller pooches have smaller emptying ducts, which the bulky secretions have been even more difficulty passed through. To make an ugly situation even uglier, if bacteria happen to work their way into the filled-up sacs, the clogged anal glands become infected, prompting abscesses.

Perianal fistulas are ulcerated sinuses located in the region around the anus, though their cause is not known. As for anal tumors, these often form near and around the anal glands, especially in older males. In fact, **perianal adenomas** are almost always found in males and are encouraged by male hormones. These tumors may produce multiple swellings around the anus and can at times be confused with an anal-gland abscess.

CARE: Take your dog to the vet, who will physically examine the area to determine the problem. Clogged anal glands can often be emptied by manually squeezing out the contents, *but this should be left to a veterinary professional!* If done incorrectly, the procedure can drive the material deeper into the anal sacs or injure the glands. If these sacs cannot be manually emptied, they may need to be flushed out using a syringe and special needle.

Abscessed anal glands are surgically opened, cleaned out, flushed of debris and swabbed with a diluted antiseptic solution. If the abscesses recur at a later date, the glands will be surgically removed.

Surgery is considered the most effective treatment of perianal fistulas. Methods used include electrosurgery, cryosurgery, and chemical cauterization, with the primary goal being the complete removal or destruction of diseased tissue while preserving normal, healthy tissue.

If your pooch has anal tumors, they will be surgically removed. Unfortunately, these growths can, and often do, recur. The majority of anal tumors are benign, but some are malignant. Cryosurgery (surgery that uses liquid nitrogen to freeze and kill the tumor) may be used in place of conventional surgery. Castration often results in the shrinking of certain types of anal tumors.

PREVENTION: Feeding your pet high-fiber dog food adds bulk to the diet, promoting larger stools and, therefore, a more-thorough emptying of the sacs with each bowel movement. This lowers the recurrence of clogged anal glands and abscesses. To keep a clogged anal gland from becoming abscessed, take your pooch to the vet if the animal begins scooting and/or licking at the anal area.

Because there is a connection between male hormone production and anal tumors, neutering your dog can prevent tumors from appearing—or reappearing.

Flatulence

Once in a while, your dog may develop gas. If this happens infrequently, something in the dog's diet may be at fault. Has your pooch been allowed to wolf down a large amount of food in a small amount of time? Has she dined on table scraps of any kind? Smaller, more frequent feedings should remedy the first situation, while limiting (or banning outright) table scraps should treat the second. The only way to prevent the possibility that your dog is getting into the garbage or neighborhood pets' dinners during her travels is to supervise all outdoor play.

But what if your dog is a more chronic gas passer? Before rushing to your vet, look at your dog's diet again. One of the most common causes of continued **flatulence** is dog food that is high in fiber, protein, or fat: If you've introduced a new food, you might consider this as the reason. Put your pooch back on her old food (or, if you switched brands for a specific reason, try yet another brand of food) for 1 week and see if the gas subsides. If this doesn't work, or if you haven't recently changed your dog's diet, there may be a gastrointestinal problem. Supplementing your dog's diet with plant-derived digestive enzymes can often solve the problem, and activated charcoal (available at your local drugstore) can absorb gas, toxins, or any other material irritating your pet's intestines (see Appendix E, List of Recommended Dosages, pp. 200–223). To help your vet diagnose a possible ailment, look for and list other symptoms before your office visit, such as a change in stool size, frequency, or consistency, a change in defecation habits, vomiting, hunched posture, or weight loss. Digestive-enzyme supplements, micronized charcoal, or *Lactobacillus* tablets may be used to help alleviate this condition.

Irregular Defecation and Feces

To know whether your pet is defecating normally, you first must know what is "normal" for your particular dog. Admittedly, this can be tough if yours is an outside pooch; somewhat easier if your pup "does her business" when you take her for daily walks.

As unpleasant as the task seems, it's important to keep informed of your dog's elimination activity. Any problems here are reliable indicators of problems within the body—typically a bacterial infection, a lodged foreign object, parasites, or an endocrine, gastric, or metabolic disorder. Worth noting are: changes in the color and/or consistency of feces, changes in frequency of elimination habits, the occurrence of obvious pain while eliminating, and the presence of blood or mucous in waste materials.

Often one of these irregularities will be the only signal that your dog's health is off. Other times your dog may also exhibit more obvious signs, such as bloating, abdominal pain, flatulence, or vomiting.

Bloody Diarrhea and General Weakness

RELATED SYMPTOMS: The dog may be losing weight despite a normal appetite and the mucous membranes may be pale.

POSSIBLE CAUSES: Did you get your puppy from a kennel or dog breeder? Have you caught your dog eating feces? Does she spend time with other canines or in areas where lots of dogs frequent? A "yes" to any of these questions may mean your dog is playing host to an internal parasite, most commonly **roundworm, hookworm,** or **whipworm.** Your pooch could have ingested the pest if she ate, licked, or sniffed an infected dog's feces. Or the larvae of a hookworm could have burrowed into your pet's skin and migrated to the intestines, where it grew into an adult and reproduced.

CARE: Take your dog—and a stool sample—to the vet. By examining the dog and performing a microscopic stool sample, your vet can reach a diagnosis. Treatment usually consists of administering a deworming medication that kills the parasites. Upgrading your pet's nutritional status to a chemical-free, high-quality diet, accompanied by digestive-enzyme supplements and antioxidant vitamins C and E, may help your dog's immune system fend off unwanted invaders (see Appendix E, List of Recommended Dosages, pp. 200–223).

PREVENTION: Puppies should receive routine deworming treatments at the following ages: 8 weeks, 12 weeks, 6 months, and 9 months. Adult dogs should have fecal exams 2 times a year.

Constant and Unsuccessful Attempts to Defecate, Accompanied by Cries of Pain and the Passing of Bloody Mucous

RELATED SYMPTOMS: The dog will also lick her anus and may vomit.

POSSIBLE CAUSE: Do you regularly give your pooch animal bones? She may suffer from **fecal impaction.** Too many bones result in rock-hard feces and painful bowel movements, which, in turn, lead to extreme constipation. In older male dogs, the situation can be made even more excruciating by an enlarged prostate that pushes against and narrows the colon. Distended or infected anal glands may predispose your pet to painful bowel movements and constipation.

CARE: Take your dog to the vet. Fecal impaction has secondary health ramifications, including anal abscesses and the poisoning of the body via metabolic by-products.

In most cases, a physical exam gives a diagnosis, while an X ray can determine the condition's severity and whether bone fragments are involved. How will your vet treat the ailment? Sometimes an enema offer is all that's needed to offer relief. Other times, the dog must be anesthetized and the bone/feces mixture removed with instruments. Any bone splinters stuck in the intestine must be extracted. One or more enemas are then given to empty the colon of the stool that has backed up.

For 2 or 3 days "post-impaction," your vet may have you mix laxatives with your dog's food to keep her stools soft. Natural laxatives you can give your dog include raw meat, psyllium, such as Metamucil (see Appendix E, List of Recommended Dosages, pp. 200–223) and mineral oil (½ to 2 teaspoons mixed with food 2 times a day for no more than 1 week). A hemorrhoidal cream (available at your local drugstore) can reduce any anal inflammation.

PREVENTION: I recommend not allowing your dog to have bones: They can present too many digestive problems. Make sure your dog is defecating regularly each day without straining. Talk to your vet about giving your dog a laxative or fecal softener if this becomes a regular problem.

Diarrhea Alternating with Constipation, Often Accompanied by Slimy Mucous and Bright Red Blood

RELATED SYMPTOMS: The dog may crouch forward and strain when defecating.

POSSIBLE CAUSE: Is your dog stressed, restless, or nervous? Do you feed her an ever-changing diet? Does she have internal parasites, such as whipworms? Has she been diagnosed with internal polyps or tumors? A "yes" to either of these may indicate **colitis**. Colitis is an inflammation of the colon's mucous lining, and it is often accompanied by ulceration. The condition can be acute (a sudden, short bout), chronic (long-term), or intermittently recurring. (Boxers seem especially susceptible to chronic colitis.) Either way, affected dogs have a loose consistency to their stools and painful bowel movements. There is usually a high frequency of defecation but small volume of feces produced.

CARE: If the condition appeared suddenly in response to a change in diet, try having your dog fast for 24 hours, but don't hold back on water. Gradually, over a 2-week period, introduce hypoallergenic, digestible foods—a mixture comprised of equal parts cottage cheese, rice, and scrambled eggs is good. Vitamin A (5,000 IU to 15,000 IU daily depending on the dog's size) has been found to help certain types of colitis (see Appendix E, List of Recommended Dosages, pp. 200–223). You can also treat your dog's diarrhea with activated charcoal (available at your local pharmacy). This helps absorb toxins, poisons, and other irritating material.

If the condition doesn't improve, visit your vet, who will ask you for a thorough history of your dog's diet and her eating and elimination habits. To rule out other conditions and identify what is causing the colitis, he will perform a stool examination and perhaps take a radiographic or perform an endoscopic exam complete with biopsy samples. Testing for food allergies may also be advised.

If your dog does have colitis, the first step involves treating the underlying factor that's causing the condition. For instance, diet-induced colitis may respond to a daily menu of high fiber, regularity-promoting food, or a hypoallergenic diet (as described above). After a 24-hour fast, a chemical-free, hypoallergenic diet can be purchased at local pet stores and used to slowly replace the dog's old diet over a 2-week period. Supplements of *Lactobacillus* bacteria (see Appendix E, List of Recommended Dosages, pp. 200–223) can be given daily to help increase the good bacteria in the colon and therefore control any pathologic bacteria that may have been producing toxins. A high-strung animal suffering from stress-generated colitis may require tranquilizers, perhaps for life.

PREVETION: Although you can do little to prevent colitis caused by polyps or tumors, you can feed your dog a consistent, high-fiber, hypoallergenic diet and limit stressful situations. Periodic stool checks and indicated wormings can prevent colitis caused by intestinal parasites such as whipworms.

No Bowel Movements, Thick Mucous in the Rectum, Vomiting, and Lack of Appetite

RELATED SYMPTOMS: Your dog is lethargic and has a painful abdomen and/or a fever. She may adopt a hunched-up stance.

POSSIBLE CAUSE: Has your dog recently ingested a small object or poisonous substance? Has she been diagnosed with a hernia, tumor, or internal parasites? If you answered "yes" to any of these, your dog may have **blocked bowels**: This typically occurs when a small portion of the intestines becomes obstructed, most often where the small and large intestines meet. The ailment can be traced to a severe gut-area inflammation, a foreign object, a hernia, a tumor, or parasites.

CARE: Take your dog to the vet immediately. If left untreated, a blocked bowel can kill the surrounding intestinal tissue and, eventually, the dog herself.

To reach a diagnosis, your vet takes a careful history, palpates her abdomen, and takes a series of X rays using oral barium as a contrast agent. If there is an obstruction, emergency surgery will clear the blockage and remove any dead tissue. Post-op care includes 2 days of intravenous feeding and 1 week's worth of antibiotics. You can also provide your dog with a soft-food diet to prevent any further straining.

PREVENTION: Watch what your dog puts in her mouth.

Recurrent Diarrhea, Itchy Anus, and Weight Loss in Spite of Normal Appetite

RELATED SYMPTOMS: The dog's coat will appear rough and dull. You may notice whitish ricelike segments—usually between ⅛- and ½-inch long—in your pet's stool and/or stuck to the hairs around the anus.

POSSIBLE CAUSE: Has your dog recently had fleas? Do you suspect she may have caught and eaten a mouse or rabbit? She may have **tapeworms.** Tapeworms are usually passed from one animal to another by fleas (who act as hosts), and enter your dog's digestive tract when the animal chews a flea that is biting her. When the dog's small intestines digest the flea, they liberate the tapeworm eggs inside. The eggs mature into adult tapeworms that attach to the lining of the digestive tract, sponging nutrients off your pet and consequently causing weight loss and, if severe, malnutrition.

CARE: Take your pet to the vet, who can deworm the animal and treat any flea infestation that may exist. You can help your pet to rid herself of the tapeworms by giving mixing her meals with either wheat-germ oil or proteolytic plant-based enzymes (see Appendix E, List of Recommended Dosages, pp. 200–223).

PREVENTION: Use a once-a-month flea preventative and stop your dog from chasing rabbits.

Checklist for Good Health

Good, illness-preventing homecare is the key to a healthy, happy pooch. Fortunately, basic health maintenance isn't hard. In fact, it's much the same for dogs as it is for humans: correct food and water intake, regular exercise, proper grooming—even checking regularly for signs of disease so that any condition can be promptly addressed and managed before it grows more serious. Here's a rundown on how to look after your pet so the two of you can enjoy a healthy, happy life together:

Normal Vital Signs

A creature's vital signs provide an important glimpse into the state of your pet's health. If your pet's vital signs differ from any of the following, there may be an underlying medical reason. Consult your vet. (See Appendix B, How to Perform a Weekly Home Exam for information on gathering this information yourself.)

Temperature: 101° to 102.5°F (29.2° to 38.3°C). Smaller dogs have slightly higher temperatures.
Resting heart rate: 75 to 120 beats per minute. Smaller dogs have slightly faster heart rates.
Resting respiration: 10 to 30 breaths per minute.

Preventive Health-Maintenance Schedule

- **Neutering (castrating/spaying):** 3 to 8 months of age.
- **Distemper-hepatitis-lepto(spirosis) vaccine:** Yearly booster* or as determined by serum titer testing.
- **Rabies vaccine:** 1- or 3-year boosters* depending on the incidence of rabies in the area. Vaccine given.
- **Kennel cough vaccine:** Yearly booster* (if you board your dog).
- **Parvovirus vaccine:** Yearly booster* or as determined by serum titer testing.
- **Lyme disease vaccine:** Yearly (if your dog gets into wooded areas) or as determined by serum titer testing.
- **Heartworm check and preventative medication:** Each spring before mosquito season begins.
- **Routine stool check:** Twice yearly.
- **Dental exam and teeth cleaning:** Every 6 to 12 months.
- **Routine physical exam:** Yearly, before 8 years of age; every 6 months after 8 years of age.
- **Routine blood screening:** Yearly, or more often if chronic disease has been previously diagnosed.

*A growing number of veterinarians are questioning the need for life-long yearly boostering. Instead, many recommend that the dog's blood be tested yearly to determine if protective levels of antibodies are present. If so, no vaccines are given. If antibody levels are low, a booster is given.

Home Emergency Kit

Should an emergency ever arise, you'll save precious time with a preassembled kit of emergency hardware. House the following essentials in a small cardboard box, fishing tackle box, or Tupperware container, and keep the kit in a convenient (yet pet-safe) location.

- Aspirin.
- Baby oil.
- Bacitracin ointment.
- Charcoal suspension.
- Chlorhexidine solution (an antiseptic).
- Cotton roll.
- Cotton swabs.
- Dramamine.
- Gauze pads (3 inch × 3 inch).
- Gauze roll (3-inch).
- Hydrogen peroxide solution (3%).
- Kaopectate.
- Muzzle.
- Milk of magnesia.
- Pepto-Bismol.
- Rectal thermometer.
- Roll of adhesive tape (1-inch).
- Rubbing alcohol.
- Scissors.
- Silver-nitrate sticks (to cauterize a bleeding nail).
- Small jar of petroleum or K-Y jelly.
- Styptic pencil.
- Tweezers.
- Wound powder or ointment.

Good Grooming

Most dogs enjoy being groomed by their owners—all that extra attention focused just on them! Such pleasure should be encouraged, because a weekly block of time set aside just for primping and pampering keeps your dog looking his very best. It also makes good health sense: by keeping hair trimmed around ears, eyes, and anus, removing matted fur, cleansing the skin, and clipping nails, you make it less likely that your dog will suffer irritation and infection.

Another benefit of good grooming is that health problems—such as parasites or a skin condition—are more quickly (and easily) noticed on a well-kept dog. You may even uncover the beginnings of a health problem while tending to your pooch. Here are a few good-grooming pointers:

EYES: It's important to keep hair out of the eyes to prevent them from becoming irritated and infected. If your pooch has long facial hair that grows into or near the eyes, be vigilant about keeping this hair clipped and out of the eyes. Any secretion buildup in the eyes can be gently removed with a soft cloth or cotton ball. To clear away hardened secretions, dampen a tissue or cloth with warm chamomile tea or water to soften the deposit and make removal easier.

EARS: Is there a buildup of earwax or dirt lining your dog's ear flap? If so, it's important to remove it. Moisten a soft cloth or tissue with baby oil and gently swipe the surface. Because dirt and wax also settle on hair that happens to be growing in the ear, you should remove strands by simply pulling them out with your fingers. Avoid trimming these hairs with scissors—you run the very real risk of shredding your pet's ear.

TEETH: To help prevent tartar buildup and gum disease, your vet may encourage you to brush the animal's teeth daily or every other day. Fortunately, this isn't difficult. Canine toothpastes are generally pleasant tasting—at least most dogs think so!—and are available from your vet or pet store. As for the toothbrush, small, rubber finger brushes are the easiest to use. Apply paste to brush and employ the same movements you use for your own teeth: small, massaging circles at the outer and inner gumlines and across the chewing surfaces.

NAILS: Too-long nails can break off or tear at the quick, causing the dog enough pain that he may refuse to walk. Thus, it's important to check your pooch's nails during each home exam. An active dog will usually inflict enough wear on his nails to keep them well-worn, but a more sedentary animal may need his claws trimmed. To do this, hold the paw horizontally. Does the tip of the nail curve below an imaginary straight line emanating from the bottom of the paw? If so, clip just that part that curves under—*no more,* since you risk cutting into the very sensitive portion of the nail that contains nerves and blood vessels. For best—and easiest—results, use a pair of dog clippers (which are available at your pet store).

COAT: How you care for your pet's coat depends greatly on what type of fur he has. Longhaired breeds should be brushed at least every other day: Begin by de-tangling hair with a wide-toothed metal comb, then finish by stroking a wire brush through the hair. For dogs with shorter fur, you can skip the detangling step and stick to once-a-week brushing.

As for bathing, unless your vet advises otherwise (or your dog gets into something and obviously needs to be washed down), once monthly is plenty. Use warm water and an extremely mild dog shampoo, available at a pet store or from your vet. *Do not use dish soap*—it is too harsh and can irritate and dry the skin. After wetting the animal's fur, pour shampoo into your hand and lather all body parts, being careful to shield the eyes. (A drop of mineral oil in each eye will help protect it from soap irritation.) Towel-dry the dog and either blow-dry fur until completely dry or keep the animal in a warm, draft-free room until the undercoat is dry.

ANUS/GENITAL REGION: A dirty hind end invites irritation, inflammation, and infection, which is why it is important to check the anal area after each walk. Should bits of feces be stuck to hair, or if the hair is soaked with urine, immediately clean the area. If your pet has long hair on his backside, you might consider clipping this fur short enough to keep it "out of the way."

Caring for a Sick Pooch

At some time in your dog's life the animal may develop a condition that requires an operation or the administration of daily medication. Here's some advice designed to help you help your pet.

GIVING PILLS: Most animals hate to swallow pills. Some pet owners have luck hiding medication in a wad of food, but others find that their cunning canines find a way to spit up the pill instead of swallowing the pill. If your pooch falls into the latter category, you can dissolve the pill's contents in liquid, then tilt the dog's head up and pour the liquid into the cheek pouch between the cheek and gums where it will be dissolved. Or, you can tilt the animal's head upward, hold open his mouth, and with your free hand, lay the pill as far back as you can on the tongue. Swiftly remove your hand from your pet's mouth and let the dog swallow. Continue to hold the dog's head in an upward tilt: This further "encourages" swallowing.

TEMPERATURE-TAKING: Rare is the dog who will hold a thermometer under his tongue. This means that if you want to take your dog's temperature, you must try another route. Enter: the rectal thermometer, an inexpensive, electronic thermometer that is safer than glass and is available at most drugstores. To use, apply a thin coating of greasy lubricant to the instrument: this can be petroleum jelly, vegetable oil, or a product such as K-Y lubricating jelly. Grasp your pet's tail with one hand and insert the thermometer with the other, slowly pushing firmly but gently. You may feel slight resistance—most likely, this means the thermometer is passing through a fecal mass.

How far the tool needs to be inserted depends on the animal's size. For a small dog, 1 inch may offer an accurate reading. For a larger dog, however, you must insert approximately ½ of the thermometer. A glass instrument should be left in for 2 minutes whereas most electronic thermometers require less than 1 minute. To read the results, roll the glass thermometer between your fingers until you can see the thin line of mercury inside or, in the case of the electronic thermometer, simply read the digital display.

MEDICATED BATHS: Skin conditions, such as eczema, and external parasites, such as fleas, ticks, and mites, require that your dog be bathed with a medicated shampoo. When using such a product, be vigilant about keeping the product out of your dog's delicate eyes and ears, and do not let your dog swallow any of the shampoo-tainted water. After lathering the product into your pooch's coat, allow it to set for 5 to 10 minutes. Rinse thoroughly with clean, warm water and towel the dog dry. As for the required frequency of medicated baths, talk to your vet. Depending on the condition being treated, every 3 days to 2 weeks is the norm.

GIVING EYEDROPS OR APPLYING OINTMENT TO THE EYE: If your dog is ever diagnosed with an eye condition, there's a good chance you'll have to administer eyedrops or ointment. To give your pooch drops, stretch the bottom lid slightly away from the eye and squeeze 3 drops inside the lid. For applying an ointment, pull out the upper eyelid slightly and squeeze a ⅓-inch strip of ointment under the lid.

CARE OF WOUNDS AND SURGICAL INCISIONS: If the wound is bandaged, leave the area alone until your vet removes the wrapping or advises you to. However, larger wounds are usually left uncovered in order to speed healing. If the wound is especially deep or infected, the vet may even insert a drain to allow fluids to escape. An uncovered incision should be kept clean by applying 3% hydrogen peroxide 2 times a day with an eye dropper or squeeze bottle. *Do not apply an ointment or any kind of lotion unless directed*—these can prevent a scab from settling over the wound.

ENEMAS: Should you need to give your dog an enema, purchase a Fleet saline or mineral oil enema from your local drugstore. Place your dog in a bathtub or take him outside, then get someone to help you restrain him (the dog will probably struggle a great deal). Be sure that his rectum and tail are exposed, then lubricate the tip of the enema bottle (if it is not a prelubricated type). Raise the dog's tail and insert the enema bottle approximately 1-inch deep into the rectum. Squeeze the contents into the dog's colon, then remove the bottle. Hold his tail down over his anus for several minutes (if possible) to keep the solution from coming out, then let your dog expel the liquid. If no bowel movement is produced, repeat.

INSULIN INJECTIONS: Should your pooch ever develop diabetes, you'll have to give him daily insulin injections. (Your vet will supply you with syringes and insulin.) Though the thought is unpleasant, the actual task isn't difficult. Start by scouting out a loose fold of skin—the neck, back, and sides of the torso are ideal. Pull up a flap of the dog's hide into a kind of tent shape. Insert the needle into the base or bottom of this "tent," making sure it has not penetrated the opposite side. Then pull back on the syringe plunger, making sure that no blood enters the syringe. If no blood appears within 2 seconds, it's okay to push the plunger in and discharge the contents of the syringe. If blood is seen in the syringe when you draw back, remove the needle and insert it at a different site. To prevent buildup of scar tissue, you must inject the insulin in a different spot each time.

How to Perform a Weekly Home Exam

Head and Neck

- **Symmetry:** Compare the features on the right side of the face with those on the left.
- **Eyes:** Check for clarity, pupil size, and excess discharge. Notice the color of the globe and inner surface of the eyelid.
- **Ears:** Learn the normal skin color. Note the odor of the ear and observe the amount of hair and wax in the canal.
- **Nose:** Check that the nostrils are open and look for any nasal discharge.
- **Mouth:** Check the color of the gums. Look for any sores and growths. Examine the teeth for tartar and look for any missing or broken teeth.
- **Trachea (windpipe):** Learn its normal size, shape, and location.
- **Lymph nodes and salivary glands:** These are located below the ears, just behind the point where the lower jaw bends vertically. Lymph nodes can also be found further down the neck, just in front of where the neck meets the body. Note any lumps or swollen nodes.
- **Thyroid gland:** Run your thumb and forefinger down either side of the windpipe, starting just below the "Adam's apple" or larynx and moving to the thoracic inlet. If the thyroid is enlarged, you may feel it

pop under your finger. If it's normal, you won't feel anything unusual.

Trunk (Body Proper)

- **Symmetry:** Compare the features on the right side with the left. Observe the degree of prominence of the ribs, hipbone, and backbone.
- **Abdomen:** Compress it with one hand on each side and note any tenseness, tenderness, or distension.
- **Mammary glands:** Note the size of the nipples and glands. Feel for lumps (in both sexes).
- **Genitals:** Examine for any swelling of the prepuce, scrotum, or vulva. Note any odor or discharge.
- **Rectal area:** Note its color and appearance. Check for fleas, tapeworm segments, dried stool, rectal protrusion, and swollen anal glands.
- **Lymph nodes:** These are located in the armpit region of the front legs and in the groin region of the back legs. Note any lumps in these areas.

Limbs

- **Symmetry:** Compare the bones and joints on the right with those on the left.
- **Gait:** Observe your pet walking and running (from several angles).
- **Anatomy:** Note the angles and relationships the bones have with one another.
- **Range of motion:** Move each joint through its full range of normal motion. Note any grating or pain the dog experiences.

Skin, Hair, Coat, and Nails

- **Skin:** Part your dog's hair and look for flakes, pimples, scales, scabs, cuts, tumors, cysts, fleas and flea stool, ticks, redness, and abrasions.
- **Hair:** Note its luster, texture, thickness, dryness, oiliness, and any areas of hair loss.

- **Nails:** Check their length and look for any split, broken, or ingrown nails.
- **Footpads:** Check for abrasions. Look between the pads for sores, foreign material, salt, and lacerations.

Pulse

- It can be easily felt in the groin at the uppermost part of the inner thigh where the leg meets the body. Note its rate, strength, and rhythm.

Heart Rate

- Place your hand on your pet's chest and feel the beat. Note the rate and rhythm.

Respiration

- Become acquainted with your pet's normal rhythmic chest motion. Note its rate and rhythm.

Eating, Drinking, Urinating, and Defecating

- Pay attention to your pet's normal motions as she performs these natural functions. Note the color, consistency, frequency, and effort of the elimination of her waste.

Posture

- Observe from several angles and note the carriage of the head, tail, and ears.

Breed Disease Predilections

Afghan Hound
- Conjunctivitis.

Airedale Terrier
- Conjunctivitis.

Basset Hound
- Conjunctivitis due to watery eyes.
- Ear infections.
- Ectropion (lower eyelid rolled outward).
- Heart disease.
- Herniated discs.
- Hip and elbow joint deformities.

Beagle
- Contact skin allergies.
- Ear infections.
- Narrowing of the pulmonary artery.
- Thyroid deficiency and hyperthyroidism.

Bernese Mountain Dog
- Age-related incontinence.
- Bone cancer.
- Conjunctivitis due to watery eyes.
- Ectropion (lower eyelid rolled outward).
- Gastric torsion.
- Heart disease.
- Herniated discs.

- Hip and elbow joint deformities.
- Vaginal prolapse during estrus.

Bloodhound
- Ear infections.

Boston Terrier
- Breathing difficulties, such as rhinitis, due to the dog's short nose.
- Difficult births/delivery due to overly large size of the puppies' heads.
- Epulis (a hard, benign overgrowth of the gums).
- Heart tumors.
- Inflammations/infections of the throat and larynx.
- Keratitis/corneal ulceration.
- Tendency to choke when excited or overheated, due to an overly narrow oral opening combined with an overly large tongue and soft palate.

Boxer
- Age-related incontinence.
- Breathing difficulties, such as rhinitis, due to the dog's short nose.
- Bone cancer.
- Contact skin allergies.
- Difficult births/delivery due to overly large size of the puppies' heads.
- Ectropion (lower eyelid rolled outward).
- Epulis (a hard, benign overgrowth of the gums).
- Heart tumors.
- Inflammations/infections of the throat and larynx.
- Inhalant skin allergies.
- Keratitis/corneal ulceration.
- Narrowing of the pulmonary artery.
- Tendency to choke when excited or overheated, due to an overly narrow oral opening combined with an overly large tongue and soft palate.

- Thyroid deficiency and hyperthyroidism.
- Urinary-tract stones.

Bulldog

- Breathing difficulties, such as rhinitis, due to the dog's short nose.
- Difficult births/delivery due to overly large size of the puppies' heads.
- Epulis (a hard benign overgrowth of the gums).
- Inflammations/infections of the throat and larynx.
- Keratitis/corneal ulceration.
- Narrowing of the pulmonary artery.
- Tendency to choke when excited or overheated, due to an overly narrow oral opening combined with an overly large tongue and soft palate.

Cairn Terrier

- Urinary-tract stones.

Chihuahua

- Collapsed windpipe due to cartilage malformation.
- Deformities of the knee and hip joints.
- Difficult pregnancy/delivery due to a narrow pelvis.
- Disease of the blood and lymph vessels.
- Narrowing of the pulmonary artery.
- Periodontosis.
- Permanent baby teeth, which often don't give way to adult teeth.

Chow Chow

- Entropion (eyelid rolled inward).

Collie

- Cataracts.
- Chronic inflammation of the cornea.
- Dermatitis of the nose due to prolonged sun exposure.
- Growth on the conjuctiva and third eyelid.
- Malformation of the aorta.

Dachshund
- Chronic inflammation of the cornea.
- Chronic valvular heart disease.
- Diabetes.
- Disease of the blood and lymph vessels.
- Epilepsy.
- Herniated discs.
- Urinary-tract stones.

Dalmatian
- Contact skin allergies.
- Urinary-tract stones.

Doberman Pinscher
- Age-related incontinence.
- Bone cancer.
- Disease of the blood and lymph vessels.
- Hemophilia.
- Thyroid deficiency.
- Vaginal prolapse during estrus.

Fox Terrier
- Chronic valvular heart disease.
- Diabetes.
- Narrowing of the pulmonary artery.

German Shepherd
- Age-related incontinence.
- Bone cancer.
- Chronic atrophy of the pancreas.
- Chronic inflammation of the cornea.
- Conjunctivitis due to watery eyes.
- Dermatitis of the nose due to prolonged sun exposure.
- Gastric torsion.
- Growth on the conjuctiva and third eyelid.
- Heart disease.
- Hemophilia.

- Herniated discs.
- Hip and elbow joint deformities.
- Inhalant skin allergies.
- Malformation of the aorta.
- Urinary-tract stones.

Golden Retriever
- Age-related incontinence.
- Cataracts.
- Hemophilia.
- Thyroid deficiency and hyperthyroidism.

Great Dane
- Age-related incontinence.
- Bone cancer.
- Conjunctivitis due to watery eyes.
- Ectropion (lower eyelid rolled outward).
- Gastric torsion.
- Heart disease.
- Herniated discs.
- Hip and elbow joint deformities.
- Vaginal prolapse during estrus.

Irish Terrier
- Urinary-tract stones.

Jack Russell Terrier
- Chronic valvular heart disease.

Labrador Retriever
- Age-related incontinence.
- Cataracts.
- Inhalant skin allergies.
- Malformation of the aorta.

Maltese
- Conjunctivitis.

Mastiff
- Age-related incontinence.
- Conjunctivitis.
- Ectropion (lower eyelid rolled outward).
- Gastric torsion.
- Heart disease.
- Herniated discs.
- Hip and elbow joint deformities.
- Tracheitis (inflammation of the windpipe) due to overly narrow windpipe.
- Vaginal prolapse during estrus.

Miniature Pinscher
- Collapsed windpipe due to cartilage malformation.
- Deformities of the knee and hip joints.
- Difficult pregnancy/delivery due to a narrow pelvis.
- Disease of the blood and lymph vessels.
- Hemophilia.
- Periodontosis.
- Permanent baby teeth, which often don't give way to adult teeth.

Miniature Schnauzer
- Collapsed windpipe due to cartilage malformation.
- Conjunctivitis.
- Deformities of the knee and hip joints.
- Difficult pregnancy/delivery due to a narrow pelvis.
- Disease of the blood and lymph vessels.
- Periodontosis.
- Permanent baby teeth, which often don't give way to adult teeth.

Miniature/Toy Poodle
- Collapsed windpipe due to cartilage malformation.
- Conjunctivitis.
- Deformities of the knee and hip joints.
- Difficult pregnancy/delivery due to a narrow pelvis.

- Disease of the blood and lymph vessels.
- Ear infections.
- Malformation of the aorta.
- Periodontosis.
- Permanent baby teeth, which often don't give way to adult teeth.
- Urinary-tract stones.

Old English Sheepdog
- Conjunctivitis.

Pekingese
- Breathing difficulties, due to the dog's short nose.
- Conjunctivitis.
- Difficult births/delivery due to overly large size of the puppies' heads.
- Epulis (a hard, benign overgrowth of the gums).
- Inflammations/infections of the throat and larynx.
- Herniated discs.
- Keratitis/corneal ulceration.
- Tendency to choke when excited or overheated, due to an overly narrow oral opening combined with an overly large tongue and soft palate.

Pit Bull Terrier
- Cataracts.
- Contact skin allergies.
- Excessive aggression.

Pomeranian
- Chronic valvular heart disease.
- Collapsed windpipe due to cartilage malformation.
- Conjunctivitis.
- Deformities of the knee and hip joints.
- Diabetes.
- Difficult pregnancy/delivery due to a narrow pelvis.
- Periodontosis.

- Permanent baby teeth, which often don't give way to adult teeth.

Poodle

- Cataracts.
- Chronic valvular heart disease.
- Conjunctivitis.
- Diabetes.
- Ear infections.
- Epilepsy.
- Herniated discs.
- Malformation of the aorta.
- Tear-staining.
- Urinary-tract stones.

Pug

- Breathing difficulties, such as rhinitis, due to the dog's short nose.
- Difficult births/delivery due to overly large size of the puppies' heads.
- Epulis (a hard, benign overgrowth of the gums).
- Inflammations/infections of the throat and larynx.
- Keratitis/corneal ulceration.
- Tendency to choke when excited or overheated, due to an overly narrow oral opening combined with an overly large tongue and soft palate.
- Urinary-tract stones.

Rottweiler

- Age-related incontinence.
- Bone cancer.
- Conjunctivitis.
- Gastric torsion.
- Heart disease.
- Herniated discs.
- Hip and elbow joint deformities.
- Vaginal prolapse during estrus.

Saint Bernard
- Age-related incontinence.
- Chronic inflammation of the cornea.
- Conjunctivitis.
- Ectropion (lower eyelid rolled outward).
- Gastric torsion.
- Heart disease.
- Herniated discs.
- Hip and elbow joint deformities.
- Vaginal prolapse during estrus.

Schnauzer
- Cataracts.
- Chronic valvular heart disease.
- Conjunctivitis.
- Disease of the blood and lymph vessels.
- Epilepsy.
- Herniated discs.

Scottish Terrier
- Hemophilia.

Setter
- Ear infections.

Shar-Pei
- Eczema between folds of skin.
- Entropion (eyelid rolled inward).
- Eye disorders and infections due to the overly narrow eye slit.

Sheltie
- Dermatitis of the nose due to prolonged sun exposure.

Shih Tzu
- Collapsed windpipe due to cartilage malformation.
- Conjunctivitis.

- Deformities of the knee and hip joints.
- Difficult pregnancy/delivery due to a narrow pelvis.
- Periodontosis.
- Permanent baby teeth, which often don't give way to adult teeth.

Siberian Husky
- Dermatitis of the nose due to prolonged sun exposure.

Spaniel
- Ear infections.
- Ectropion (lower eyelid rolled outward).
- Herniated discs.

Toy Yorkshire Terrier
- Collapsed windpipe due to cartilage malformation.
- Conjunctivitis.
- Deformities of the knee and hip joints.
- Difficult pregnancy/delivery due to a narrow pelvis.
- Disease of the blood and lymph vessels.
- Periodontosis.
- Permanent baby teeth, which often don't give way to adult teeth.

Welsh Corgi
- Herniated discs.

Welsh Terrier
- Diabetes.

Important Questions to Answer Before Going in for an Exam

1. What is the major health concern that brought you and your pet to the clinic? What other minor concerns do you have?
2. When did you first notice something was wrong?
3. What was the first sign of illness you observed?
4. List, in order of time of appearance, the other symptoms you have noticed. Which of these symptoms are still present? Have they improved, gotten worse, or remained the same?
5. Have you done anything at home to treat the problem?
6. How is the animal's appetite, thirst, urination, defecation, and activity?
7. Have you noticed any changes in your dog's behavior, movement, or breathing?
8. If there is lameness, be sure you know which leg has been favored at home.
9. Has your pet been to another veterinarian for the same problem? If so, what tests did he perform and what were the results? What was his diagnosis? Was medication dispensed? If so, what kind and did it help?

List of Recommended Dosages

How to Use This Chart

The doses of vitamins, minerals, herbs, and enzymes listed here are in some cases higher than the scientifically determined daily requirements that are recommended for a healthy diet. Many of the vitamin and mineral dosages listed here are megadoses used to support the body in fighting off disease threats and not simply for preventing vitamin and mineral deficiencies. Scientifically determined animal doses for herbs are not available; therefore, the herb doses recommended here are strictly "anecdotal"—meaning doses that Dr. Simon and other veterinary practitioners have determined from personal clinical experience. Every attempt has been made to be cautious and safe in such recommendations; however, individual pet owners must decide whether to use such dosage information to treat their dogs. Although Dr. Simon uses these dosages in his own practice, be aware that individual sensitivities and allergic reactions are always possible. If your pet develops any adverse symptoms shortly after beginning such supplements, discontinue using the supplements and call your veterinarian for advice. The doses provided here are for treating a current condition, and generally are not intended for long-term supplementation.

*When doses listed here are based on a specific body weight, adjust the dose according to your dog's size (for example, if a 20-pound dog would get 200 mg of a substance, a 10-pound dog would get 100 mg and a 60-pound dog would get 600 mg). **At no time should a dog get more than the recommended adult human dose.**

	Description	Dosages
Activated charcoal suspension (also known as micronized charcoal)	Absorbs toxins; used to treat ingestion of poison	3 to 6 ml per pound given orally; repeat dose in 1 hour
Aspirin (baby) or Bufferin	Pain reliever	5 to 12 mg per pound given orally every 8 to 12 hours
Benadryl	Antihistamine	1 to 2 mg per pound given orally every 6 to 8 hours

Where to Find	Additional Info
Ask your pharmacist or veterinarian to order it for you	
Drugstores	Never use in conjunction with cortisone (steroids) or if a bleeding disorder is present; should not be used post-surgically due to anticlotting effects; long-term use can lead to gastric irritation, ulceration, and bleeding
Drugstores	

	Description	Dosages
Beta-carotene	Beta-carotene is a precursor to vitamin A; it is converted to vitamin A by the dog's body and is not toxic, so it can be given safely in place of vitamin A, which can be toxic in high doses	A 20-pound dog should be given daily a dose of beta-carotene equivalent to 10,000 IU of vitamin A for short-term use; for long-term use, a 20-pound dog should be given daily a dose of beta-carotene equivalent to 1,000 IU of vitamin A
Chlorphenira-mine	Antihistamine	A 20-pound dog should be given 2 mg orally every 8 to 12 hours; at no time should the dose exceed 12 mg.

Where to Find	Additional Info
Drugstores or health-food stores	
Drugstores or your veterinarians' offices	A good brand name to look for is Chlor-Trimeton

	Description	Dosages
Chondroitin sulfate	A naturally occurring compound made up of a combination of protein and carbohydrates; protects joints and can be used to treat arthritis	A 50-pound dog should be given 1,000 mg daily
Cod liver oil	Used to treat corneal ulcers and/or erosions	1 drop in affected eye daily
Colloidal silver	A suspension of tiny silver particles in water	For topical use on burns and wounds, use as a flushing preparation 3 times a day
Cranberry	Herb used to treat urinary-tract problems	A 20-pound dog should be given 1/4 of the recommended adult human dose

Where to Find	Additional Info
Health-food stores, veterinarian's office, and some drugstores	Often used in combination with glucosamine sulfate; if using both, give your dog half doses of each
Drugstores	Before treating, check with your vet: corneal ulcers and erosions can be quite dangerous, so it is best to use this treatment with veterinary supervision
Health-food stores and veterinarian's office	
Health-food stores	Best used in tablet form

	Description	Dosages
Dandelion	Herb with diuretic properties used to help reduce pulmonary congestion	A 20-pound dog should be given 1/4 the recommended adult human dose
Dimethylglycine	Vitaminlike supplement that can be used as an immune stimulant	A dog under 25 lbs. should get 50 mg.; between 26 and 50 lbs. should get 100 mg; between 51 and 90 lbs. should get 150 mg; over 90 lbs. should get 200 mg; **see additional info column**
Echinacea	Herb used to promote healing of wounds and improve immune system	A 20-pound dog should be given 1/8 of the recommended adult human dose; use at 10-day intervals, separated by a 7-day rest; stop use after 3 10-day trials

Where to Find	Additional Info
Health-food stores	Best used in tablet form
Health-food stores	Because different companies use different concentrations of dimethylglycine in their solutions, you must check the concentration of milligrams per milliliter listed on the bottle and calculate the number of milliliters to give your dog
Health-food stores	Obtain organic freeze-dried sources when possible

	Description	**Dosages**
Flaxseed oil	Herbal oil that encourages healthy skin and a full hair coat; a natural anti-inflammatory agent and immune modulator	A 20-pound dog should be given the equivalent of 1/4 to 1/2 of the recommended adult human dose
Gatorade	Sugar and electrolyte drink; can be used to prevent dehydration when treating repetitive vomiting and diarrhea	Put 1/4-inch in bowl in place of water; when dog empties bowl, wait 20 minutes, then place another 1/4-inch in bowl; repeat until vomiting subsides
Glucosamine sulfate	A naturally occurring compound made up of a combination of protein and carbohydrates; protects joints and can be used to treat arthritis	A 50-pound dog should be given 1,000 mg daily

Where to Find	Additional Info
Drugstores or health-food stores	Keep refrigerated so that the oil doesn't become rancid; purchase a human-grade, organic, cold-pressed form of the oil, preferably in gelatin capsules
Grocery store	
Health-food stores, veterinarians' offices, and some drugstores	Often used in combination with chondroitin sulfate; if using both, give the dog half doses of each

	Description	**Dosages**
Iodine	Mineral that prevents goiter (enlargement of the thyroid gland)	A 20-pound dog should be given 1/8 of the recommended adult human dose
Kaopectate	Absorbent used to treat diarrhea and vomiting	0.5 to 1.0 ml per pound given orally every 2 to 6 hours
Lactobacillus	The ''good'' bacteria naturally present in the intestines of healthy animals that controls the ''bad'' bacteria and yeast; synthesizes B vitamins and provides the cells of the intestinal lining with fatty acids	A 20-pound dog should be given 1/4 of the recommended adult human dose

Where to Find	Additional Info
Health-food stores and some drugstores	Give in the form of kelp tablets
Drugstores	
Drugstores, health-food stores, and vet's office	When purchasing, opt for high-quality brand-name products that are stored in refrigerated areas of the store in order to ensure that the viability of the live bacteria is maintained

	Description	**Dosages**
Lecithin	A fat found in animal and plant tissue; used to help strengthen the sphincter muscle of the bladder; also aids in promoting mental alertness in old animals	A 20-pound dog should be given 1/4 of the recommended adult human dose of soy lecithin oil daily
Licorice root	Herb that acts as a natural cortisone; helpful in reducing throat swelling and inflammation of the stomach	A 20-pound dog should be given 1/8 of the recommended adult human dose
Metamucil (Psyllium husks, not seed)	Natural source of fiber that acts as a bulk cathartic and prevents and treats constipation	A 20-pound dog should be given 1/4 of the recommended adult human dose
Milk thistle	Herb that contains antioxidants important for maintaining a healthy liver	A 20-pound dog should be given 1/4 of the recommended adult human dose

Where to Find	Additional Info
Health-food stores.	Buy fresh bottles of lecithin sold in refrigerated areas; it is important to keep it refrigerated to avoid getting rancid
Health-food stores	Do not use for longer than 10 days
Drugstore, health-food stores, and veterinarians' offices	It's very important to increase your pet's water consumption when supplying psyllium; if no bowel movement is produced in 48 hours, see your veterinarian
Health-food stores	

	Description	Dosages
Parsley	Diuretic herb that can help reduce pulmonary congestion	A 20-pound dog should be given 1/4 of the recommended adult human dose
Pedialyte	Pediatric electrolyte solution that can help to treat eclampsia and vomiting	A 20-pound dog should be given 1/2 the recommended children's dose
Pepto-Bismol	Antidiarrheal agent that also soothes the stomach	0.5 to 1.5 ml per pound given orally every 2 to 6 hours for short-term use (1 or 2 days)
Plant-derived digestive-enzyme supplements	A source of enzymes that helps the body to digest its food	A 20-pound dog should be given 1/4 of the recommended adult human dose; dose should be sprinkled over lightly dampened food 10 minutes before it is served

Where to Find	Additional Info
Health-food stores	Best to get in tablet form
Drugstores	
Drugstores	Use only for 1 or 2 days; if symptoms continue, seek veterinarian's advice. Be aware that it may cause the dog's stool to turn black, which is often confused with blood in the stool
Health-food stores	Buy a brand name for humans unless a pet supplement is available; the supplement should contain amylase, protease, lipase, and cellulase

	Description	Dosages
Proteolytic enzyme supplement	A specific type of digestive enzyme supplement that contains only protease	A 20-pound dog should be given 1/2 of the recommended adult human dose
Robitussin DM	Cough suppressant	0.25 to 1 ml per pound given orally every 6 to 8 hours
Selenium	Mineral used for protecting the immune system; helpful for maintaining healthy heart, joints, and muscles	A 20-pound dog should be given no more than 30 mcg daily without a veterinarian's recommendation
Shark cartilage	Natural anti-inflammatory for arthritis treatment	A 40-pound dog should be given 1/3 of the recommended adult human dose
Sulfur	Mineral required for synthesis of body proteins; can also act as an antioxidant	500 mg in the form of methylsulfonyl methane per 30 pounds daily

Where to Find	Additional Info
Health-food stores	For most effective results, give apart from meals; bromelain or papäin tablets are recommended
Drugstores	Because it merely subdues symptoms and makes the animal more comfortable, do not use for more than 4 days without a veterinarian's advice; you could be covering up a more serious problem
Drugstores or health-food stores	Because it is toxic in high doses, be sure that you are not also providing selenium with any other supplements (or *only* give in a combination tablet; see **"Vitamin E"**)
Vet's office or health-food store	Available in tablet or powder form
Health-food stores	Purchase in form of methylsulfonyl methane

	Description	Dosages
Trace mineral supplements	Essential minerals that keep the body functioning properly	A 20-pound dog should be given 1/4 of the recommended adult human dose
Valerian	Herb used for its sedative properties; reduces anxiety and helps to treat muscle spasms	A 20-pound dog should be given 1/8 of the recommended adult human dose
Vitamin A	See **Beta-carotene**	
Vitamin B complex	Vitamin that helps to maintain healthy nerves, skin, eyes, hair, liver, and mouth	Follow dose recommended on a bottle of a brand made especially for pets
Vitamin C	Vitamin used for strengthening the immune system; also, an anti-allergic, anti-inflammatory, anti-bacterial, antiviral, and detoxicant agent	500 mg per 20 pounds daily; reduce the dose if a soft stool develops

Where to Find	Additional Info
Health-food stores	Best form to purchase is chelated trace mineral tablets that contain as many as 74 different trace minerals
Health-food stores (in pill form)	If this dose does not produce acceptable results, double the dose and evaluate the effect; valerian has a bad taste, so mix it with your dog's food to mask the taste
Pet stores or veterinarians' offices	Your vet will be able to recommend a brand made specifically for pets
Drugstores or health-food stores	Best purchased in calcium ascorbate or sodium ascorbate forms rather than acidic acid form, which can upset the stomach; try to obtain a brand that includes bioflavonoids

	Description	Dosages
Vitamin E	Essential antioxidant vitamin used for strengthening the immune system	A 20-pound dog should be given 200 IU daily when treating a health problem
Zinc	Essential mineral used for tissue repair and healing, proper immune-system functioning, and healthy skin and coat	A 20-pound dog should be given 10 mg daily; dogs under 20 pounds should be given 5 mg daily; dogs over 40 pounds or over should be given 15 to 20 mg daily

Where to Find	Additional Info
Drugstores or health-food stores	Because it is a fat-soluble substance that accumulates in the body, it can become toxic in high doses (see also **Selenium;** you may want to purchase vitamin E with selenium in a combination tablet in order to add a safe dose of selenium to your dog's diet)
Drugstores, health-food stores, or veterinarians' offices	Absorbed most efficiently if purchased in its chelated form; potentially toxic in high doses, so be sure you are not supplying it in any other supplements; take with a copper supplement, because it may interfere with absorption of naturally occurring copper

Index

About the Authors

JOHN M. SIMON, DVM, owns a private practice, Woodside Animal Hospital, in Royal Oak, Michigan. A graduate of the Michigan State University School of Veterinary Medicine, Dr. Simon has over thirty years of experience in conventional and alternative pet care. In 1982, Dr. Simon became Detroit's first certified veterinary acupuncturist; in 1996, he received his certificate from the American Veterinary Chiropractic Association. Dr. Simon is a past president of the Oakland County Veterinary Medical Association (OCVMA) and has served as both an officer and board member of the Southeastern Michigan Veterinary Medical Association (SEMVMA). In 1993, he began hosting his own weekly cable TV talk show entitled *Your Pet's Good Health.* Author of *Basic Bird Care & Preventive Medicine,* Dr. Simon has written a regular column in Detroit's *Daily Tribune* since 1983 and has contributed extensively to pet-care magazines such as *Natural Pet.* His practice has been featured on both the local and national television news. Dr. Simon lives in Franklin Village, Michigan, with his wife and two children.

STEPHANIE PEDERSEN is a freelance writer and editor who specializes in the areas of health and beauty. Her articles have appeared in numerous publications, including *American Woman, Sassy, Teen, Unique Homes, Weight Watchers,* and *Woman's World.* She has also cowritten *What Your Cat Is Trying to Tell You: A Head-to-Tail Guide to Your Cat's Symptoms—and Their Solutions* with Dr. Simon. She currently resides in New York City.